Writing Successful Undergraduate Diss in Social Sciences

A practical guide for students undertaking their dissertation, *Writing Successful Undergraduate Dissertations in Social Sciences* uses a mixture of exercises, strategies, case study material and further reading to give hints and tips on beginning and managing a research project and working with supervisors.

Providing an accessible overview of the essential steps in conducting research and writing dissertations, this fully updated edition contains new sections on:

- The varied sources of support for students and how to make use of them
- The use of modern technologies and digital platforms in data collection, storage and processing
- The important issues relating to ethnographic and feminist research
- How to publish through peer review publications or using self-publishing platforms
- The General Data Protection Regulation and legal issues relating to collection, storage and use of personal data
- The skills that students have acquired through writing dissertations and how those skills could become useful for future career and employability
- How students can relate their dissertations to existing theories and concepts in social sciences that relate to their dissertation.

Packed with proven practical advice from 'real-life' data, case studies and examples, *Writing Successful Undergraduate Dissertations in Social Sciences* is an essential and dependable starting point and guide for any student beginning their dissertation journey in the social sciences.

Francis Jegede is Associate Professor in International Relations and Diplomacy and Chair of the College Research Committee, College of Business, Law and Social Sciences, University of Derby, UK.

Charlotte Hargreaves is the Head of Criminology and Social Sciences at the University of Derby, UK.

Karen Smith leads Collaborative Research and Development in the School of Education at the University of Hertfordshire, UK.

Philip Hodgson is the Head of the School of Law and Social Sciences at the University of Derby, UK.

Malcolm J. Todd is Professor of Sociology and the Deputy Vice Chancellor and Provost at the University of Derby, UK. He is a National Teaching Fellow and has written widely on learning and teaching in higher education.

Julia Waldman has left academia and is now Film Production and Business Manager for Robin Creative Media.

Writing Successful Undergraduate Dissertations in Social Sciences

A Student's Handbook

Second Edition

Francis Jegede, Charlotte Hargreaves, Karen Smith, Philip Hodgson, Malcolm J. Todd and Julia Waldman

Routledge
Taylor & Francis Group

LONDON AND NEW YORK

Second edition published 2020
by Routledge
2 Park Square, Milton Park, Abingdon, Oxon, OX14 4RN

and by Routledge
52 Vanderbilt Avenue, New York, NY 10017

Routledge is an imprint of the Taylor & Francis Group, an informa business

© 2020 Francis Jegede, Charlotte Hargreaves, Karen Smith, Philip Hodgson, Malcolm J. Todd and Julia Waldman

First edition published by Routledge 2009

British Library Cataloguing-in-Publication Data
A catalogue record for this book is available from the British Library

Library of Congress Cataloging-in-Publication Data
A catalog record has been requested for this book

ISBN: 978-0-367-25523-7 (hbk)
ISBN: 978-0-367-25525-1 (pbk)
ISBN: 978-0-429-28825-8 (ebk)

Typeset in Garamond
by Swales & Willis, Exeter, Devon, UK

MIX
Paper from
responsible sources
FSC
www.fsc.org   FSC™ C013985

Printed in the United Kingdom
by Henry Ling Limited

This edition is dedicated to my children: Panashe and Cecilia. Thanks as ever to my husband, Chidochangu, for his patience.

Karen Smith

This book is dedicated to all the students that I have had the privilege to teach, supervise, nurture or inspire along the way in my academic career and to my family for their love, understanding and patience in my endless quest for knowledge.

Francis Jegede

This book is dedicated to my two beautiful children: Izzy and Immy. As always, my wife Sally is incredibly supportive of my work and I truly thank her.

Malcolm J. Todd

This edition is dedicated to my grandchildren Evie, Eliana, Harry and Molly.

Julia Waldman

Contents

Figures, tables and case studies

Figures

Tables

Case studies

Contributors

Francis Jegede is Associate Professor in International Relations and Diplomacy in the College of Law, Humanities and Social Sciences at the University of Derby. He is the Chair of the College Research Committee. Francis has had a long service at the University of Derby as Subject and Programme Leader for International Relations and Diplomacy. His research interests include international development, security, terrorism, diplomacy and international institutions. He has well-developed research and educational links with international institutions such as the United Nations, the European Union and international NGOs. He has extensive experience in supervising undergraduate dissertations and has led research trips to a number of countries in Europe, Africa and Asia.

Charlotte Hargreaves is the Head of Criminology and Social Sciences at the University of Derby. She is an experienced researcher and prior to entering academia worked for the National Foundation for Educational Research. While she has worked on a number of research projects and has published widely, her primary research interest focuses on young people. She is an expert in qualitative research methods and undertaking research with hard to reach groups.

Karen Smith is Principal Lecturer in Collaborative Research and Development in the School of Education at the University of Hertfordshire, where she leads research and evaluation projects with external partners and is Director of the Professional Doctorate in Education. Karen's research interests relate to how higher education policies and practices impact on those who work and study within the university system. Her work has focused specifically on transnational educators, international students, educational developers and innovative practitioners and has demonstrated how their experience of university is shaped by its policies, procedures and initiatives.

Philip Hodgson is the Head of the School of Law and Social Sciences at the University of Derby. He has extensive experience of supervising research projects with students and has previously taught research methods at undergraduate level. Prior to entering academia, he worked in a number of roles within the criminal justice system and he is particularly interested in relating theory to practice. He has been involved in, and led on, a number of research projects mainly focusing on policing, young people, drugs and social exclusion.

Malcolm J. Todd is the Provost at the University of Derby. He is a National Teaching Fellow and has published widely in the areas of learning and teaching.

Julia Waldman worked in universities for 16 years; as a Senior Research Fellow, undertaking research mainly related to children and young people; as a lecturer; in programme development; supervising many students' dissertations; and for the HEA. She published widely on the use of new technologies in teaching and learning. She then returned to practice, working in senior management in children's services for many years. She now works as Production and Business Manager for Robin Creative Media, a video production company.

Acknowledgements

This first edition of this book grew out of an online resource, *The Companion for Undergraduate Dissertations*, developed by Malcolm Todd and Julia Waldman and the Higher Education Academy's Subject Centres for Sociology, Anthropology and Politics (C-SAP) and Social Work and Policy (SWAP) and including the contributions of many other contributors. We would like to acknowledge C-SAP and SWAP's support for our work and, in particular, that of Helen Howard and Anthony Rosie from C-SAP who made resources available to develop the online support and Jackie Rafferty of SWAP.

We would also like to recognise the contributions of Ian Baker, Jenny Blain, Sue Hemmings, Anne Hollows, Ann Macaskill, Darren Marsh, Ruth McManus, Liam Mellor, Janet Morton, Andy Pilkington, Gary Taylor, John Steel and Christopher Winch. Their work, which originally appeared in *The Companion*, has helped to shape much of the original book.

The following people also contributed many of the insightful quotes and case studies in the book: Mike Bracher, Iain Garner, Caroline Gibson, Marcus Green, Catherine Hanley, Katherine Harrington, Cath Lambert, Sarah Lynch, Tsang Kwok Kuen, David Metcalfe, Peter O'Neill, Gillian Ruch, Beverley Searle, Becky Webb, Kanishka Wattage and Alan McGauley.

We are also indebted to the critical friends who gave us insightful feedback on draft chapters of the first edition. They are: Sean Demack, Scott Fernie, Carol Hayden, Jessica Henderson, Martina Johnson, Liz Lawrence, Colin McCaig, Darren Marsh, Marian Morris, Nick Pilcher, Jackie Powell, Steve Spencer, Viv Thom, Cal Weatherald and Rose Wiles.

We would like to thank Carfax Publishing Company, part of the Taylor & Francis Group, for permission to cite from: Todd, M.,

Bannister, P. and Clegg, S. 'Independent inquiry and the undergraduate dissertation: perceptions and experiences of final-year social science students', *Assessment and Evaluation in Higher Education*, 29 (3) June 2004. We would also like to thank Routledge for permission to cite from: Todd, M.J., Smith, K. and Bannister, P. 'Staff Experiences and Perceptions of Supervising a Social Science Undergraduate Dissertation', *Teaching in Higher Education*, 11 (2) 2006. QAA for the reproduction of Figure 12.1

In preparation for the second edition, we extend our thanks to Dr John Stubbs for reading through the draft chapters and for offering some useful comments. Thanks are also due to him and all the reviewers of the manuscript proposal for their insights that fed into this edition.

We also recognise the editorial team at Routledge: Sarah Tuckwell and Lisa Font.

But our biggest thanks go to our social science dissertation students whose experiences motivated us to write the original book and to prepare the second edition a decade later.

Preface

As undergraduate social science students, for many of you a significant part of your final-year study at college or university will focus on an independent learning project. The name for this project may vary from institution to institution and from country to country: in some places, in the UK, for example, it could be called a 'dissertation'; elsewhere it could be described as an 'extended essay' or 'final-year project'. Whichever way your own institution describes it, we are aware that the dissertation can demand a great deal from you (synthesising theory, selecting and applying methodology, conducting research and analysing data, etc.) and that many of you may not feel fully prepared for this form of assessment. We have tried, therefore, to write a book for you in an approachable and accessible style, one that provides you with support and guidance to help you through the dissertation process.

Our aims

This book is the revised and updated edition of *Doing Your Undergraduate Social Science Dissertation* book, first published in 2009. Following the success of the first edition, this second edition has now been revised and supplemented with updated information and ideas to help you write a successful dissertation. The original authors, Julia Waldman, Malcolm Todd and Karen Smith, have been joined in this new edition by Francis Jegede, Charlotte Hargreaves and Philip Hodgson, who bring with them many years' experience of supervision, research methods teaching and research within the social sciences.

This new edition takes account of and relates to current pedagogy of teaching research methods and reflects the changing techniques and ways you as a student will learn, undertake fieldwork and write a dissertation. The topics and themes covered in this new edition are relevant to contemporary social, economic and political issues in society as these influence the nature of data that you will collect in order to undertake your undergraduate research.

The book offers new sources of information and covers new ways you can interact with and collect data using new technologies and social media platforms. In addition to offering you a guide to the dissertation process, this revised edition offers practical exercises with case studies to assist you in your study. You can apply its user-friendly presentation with schematic diagrams of key points to your undergraduate research project or dissertation.

The 'key messages' and 'key questions' sections of the book include specific tasks that you need to undertake in relation to your dissertation as part of a productive learning activity. The key questions and activities in each chapter also relate to specific case studies to enable you to link theories, concepts and research ideas to real-life situations.

As a textbook on 'doing a dissertation', with sections on 'on what do' and 'what not to do' in a dissertation, it identifies common mistakes that you may make while doing your project. Written by experienced academics, the book is based on authors' synthesis of 'feedback' they have provided to students in the course of their role as dissertation supervisors and postgraduate research managers. In addition, the authors have substantial research and publication experience and have undertaken successful research projects, some of which will be offered as examples throughout the text. Two of the authors have researched staff experience of supervising final-year students, and have published findings in international learning and teaching journals. All the authors have a long-standing and wide research interest in understanding how students learn and how, as teachers, educators and researchers they can look at ways of supporting students to achieve their own full potential. The book is, therefore, informed by research and is evidence based.

Given its contents, type of presentation and practical guide, we expect the book to be one that you may wish to use as a source book to enable you to respond to some of the frequent questions, concerns and practical issues you may encounter when preparing for and completing your dissertation or final-year project.

The revised edition retains a strongly student-centred stance. We, the authors, recognise that there are many ways in which the 'journey' through the process of writing a successful dissertation can be completed. So, we have written this book as a dependable resource to help you start on your dissertation journey and to offer you guidance along the way to the completion of your dissertation.

The book should be supplemented by discussions with your supervisors, your fellow students and information provided by your university. In addition, there are many other resources and sources of information which you can and should access, some of which we identify in the further reading. We believe that students should aim to become effective, independent and self-confident learners, who can make informed decisions about their own learning. We strongly believe that this is a key characteristic of becoming an autonomous learner, and we hope that the book will contribute, in some way, to that aim. Importantly, we want to help you have success in writing your dissertation and hope this book will help achieve this.

How to use this book

It is intended that the book should be useful in the preparation period when you're thinking about the focus of your dissertation, research design, collection of data and their analysis and throughout your final year – right up to submitting the final project and what happens afterwards. The chapters will follow a sequence that is designed to help you through a number of these key stages. But we have also designed the book so it can be used in a more flexible way and be adaptable as your own needs change. For example, before you start the dissertation, you can use it to:

- Explore the demands of a dissertation
- Raise questions that you can ask your supervisor
- Help you think through what theme you could pursue in your dissertation
- Help you prepare a research question.

If you have already started the dissertation, you can also use it to:

- Clarify issues about specific chapters of the dissertation
- Focus on specific aspects of the study, e.g. ethical issues or research methodology
- Organise the different stages of the dissertation.

Each chapter contains helpful guidance on how to progress through each stage of the process. There is a series of case studies which we hope will provide a helpful way for you to better understand your dissertation journey. Each chapter concludes with a set of key messages and key questions. These are provided to assist you with reflecting upon what you have gained from each chapter and what action you may need to take your own dissertation forward.

Concluding comments

We hope that this book will offer you some practical support along your learning journey, and we welcome feedback from you on how we might be able to improve future editions of this book.

Chapter 1

What is a dissertation?

Introduction

This chapter explores what a dissertation or final-year project is, in order to better understand the distinctive features of this form of assessment within the undergraduate degree programme. It explains why a dissertation is required in undergraduate study and highlights the ways in which the dissertation differs to other modules you may have taken previously due to the emphasis it places upon you to take much more responsibility for your own learning. Ultimately, it provides an opportunity for you to produce your own unique piece of work. Some dissertations can even be published and start you on your own academic career. By the end of this chapter, you will have a better understanding of the following:

- What a dissertation is
- Why the dissertation is essential to your undergraduate degree programme
- What makes a dissertation special
- What a dissertation may look like
- How to prepare for and approach a dissertation.

Definitions of the dissertation

For many undergraduate social science degree students, a significant element of final-year study is an independent learning project, generally known as a dissertation. A dissertation has been defined in different ways by different people as shown in Figure 1.1. In this book we call the project a 'dissertation', but other terms, including 'extended essay',

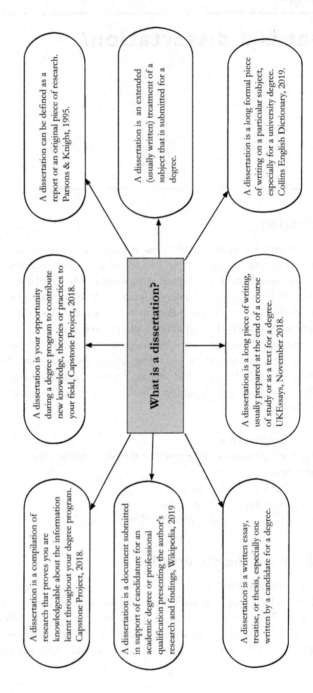

Figure 1.1 What is a dissertation?

What is a dissertation?

A dissertation can be defined as a report or an original piece of research. Parsons & Knight, 1995.

A dissertation is an extended (usually written) treatment of a subject that is submitted for a degree.

A dissertation is a long formal piece of writing on a particular subject, especially for a university degree. Collins English Dictionary, 2019.

A dissertation is your opportunity during a degree program to contribute new knowledge, theories or practices to your field, Capstone Project, 2018.

A dissertation is a long piece of writing, usually prepared at the end of a course of study or as a text for a degree. UKEssays, November 2018.

A dissertation is a compilation of research that proves you are knowledgeable about the information learnt throughout your degree program. Capstone Project, 2018.

A dissertation is a document submitted in support of candidature for an academic degree or professional qualification presenting the author's research and findings, Wikipedia, 2019

A dissertation is a written essay, treatise, or thesis, especially one written by a candidate for a degree.

'thesis', 'independent learning project', 'capstone project', 'senior paper' or 'final-year project' are also used. While these projects may vary greatly in scope and nature (e.g. a large-scale written assignment such as a dissertation or extended essay or the design and production of some type of artefact, posters, exhibitions etc.), most share a number of key characteristics (Todd et al. 2004).

1. The learner determines the focus and direction of their work.
2. This work is carried out on an individual basis – although usually with some tutor support and direction provided.
3. There is typically a substantial research component to the project, requiring the collection of primary data, the analysis of existing/secondary data or both.
4. Learners will have a more prolonged engagement with the chosen subject than is the case with 'standard' coursework assignments such as essays or reports, with the work consequently expected to be more in-depth.

Purpose of a dissertation

In many universities, the dissertation project can be a significant influencing factor in determining students' final degree classification as it often carries more weighting than a traditional module. Although undertaking a dissertation is an essential requirement of most undergraduate degrees, the choice of subject covered by the dissertation can be influenced by different reasons. For example, people may choose specific topics or areas because of their curiosity, personal experience or circumstances. Ultimately, however, the purpose of undertaking a dissertation can generally be summarised as the desire to:

1. Undertake a scientific enquiry or investigation into something with a view of discovering new facts or ideas
2. Evaluate the impact or effect of something or a particular phenomenon
3. Establish the truths in or validity of a claim or theories or laws
4. Find out if and how something works by collecting relevant information about a particular subject
5. Improve personal or professional skills and development in social research and investigation

6. Develop your subject expertise and intellectual and organisational skill
7. Provide a scoping exercise for post graduate study.

Depending on the purpose, key types of questions that dissertations tend to answer are:

1. What is the situation with a particular social, economic, political or cultural issue?
2. How are things related in terms of structures, connections and relationships?
3. What happens why, when, where and how?

Once the topic of investigation is decided and the purpose of doing your dissertation is established, your ideas need to be shaped into a more specific research question(s). These questions need to be clearly stated in terms of aims and objectives. The more specific your research questions, the more focused your study will be and therefore it will be easier for you to reach conclusions based on the analysis of your data.

What distinguishes the dissertation from other work?

More than any other undergraduate assessed work, the dissertation offers you the opportunity to further develop your subject expertise and your social research, intellectual and organisational skills. The dissertation gives you a unique opportunity to work in considerable detail on a topic of special interest to you. It requires you becoming more actively involved with research, this could mean empirical research or a library-based project. It provides more scope for originality and intellectual independence than you have perhaps experienced before.

Your first essays were usually (though not always) written to titles that had been prescribed by your tutor. As you progressed through your course, you may have been given the opportunity to design your own assignment questions. In this way your independence, as a reader and critic, will have developed. Similarly, you may have noticed that you no longer read books and papers simply to understand them and re-present their arguments in an essay. Rather, you notice what particularly interested you in the books, journal articles or media sources and what particular critical questions you wanted to ask about them. The dissertation builds on this foundation; it grows out of your own particular interest, both in terms of the material you choose to write about and the topic that provides the focus of your study.

The longer word count of the dissertation requires you to sustain your analysis and interpretation over a greater range of material and almost inevitably involves you in more careful and subtle argument and critical evaluation. The preparation and writing of the dissertation make you take responsibility, with the support of a tutor or supervisor, for your own learning. You have to manage your independent study, your time and present the results of research clearly and methodically. You need to remember that the dissertation is a marathon rather than a sprint!

In many ways, the dissertation is about *doing* social science rather than writing about the social science research that others have produced. You will develop skills that will improve your expertise at subject level and be expected to collect and manipulate information, present and demonstrate critical thinking and problem-solving skills – all of which will be beneficial for your professional life or in preparing you for study at postgraduate level.

For these reasons, the dissertation can be seen as the culmination of your undergraduate studies, honing your academic skills and presenting ideas which are uniquely your own.

Dissertation organisation and structure

The way in which this type of assessment is organised will vary from institution to institution and programme to programme. It is therefore important that you familiarise yourself with the particular arrangements for your degree. Many institutions produce module guidance setting out these requirements and also will allocate students a dissertation tutor or supervisor. Your supervisor, and any guidance which is offered, should be your primary sources of information and support for the dissertation project. While this book provides an overarching guide to the dissertation process, ultimately you will be assessed on the requirements of your own university and although most universities have a standard requirement of 'an introduction, a literature review, methodology, findings, conclusion and bibliographic references', there may be slight differences that you need to be aware of.

It is worth being very clear from the earliest planning stages of your dissertation exactly what is being asked of you. Questions that you should be asking yourself include:

- If required, have I sought and obtained ethical approval for my research?
- How many credits does the dissertation carry?
- How many words do I have to write?
- How often can I meet my supervisor?
- What can I expect from my supervisor and what should my supervisor expect from me?
- Are there any interim progress reports or oral presentations that I need to provide for my institution/supervisor as part of my assessment?
- What are the submission points and in what format?
- What system of referencing and citations am I required to use?
- What deadline am I working to and how can I manage my time to ensure completion by the deadline?

As the sayings go, 'poor planning makes poor performance' and 'failing to plan is planning to fail', so good planning and preparation in the early stages are essential for writing a successful dissertation.

All dissertations will vary in format, style and design; however, a dissertation generally contains four main sections (Swales and Feak 2004: 222):

1. Introductory section that sets out the context, aim and objective of your study;
2. Methodology section that provides information on how and why you conducted your research;
3. Findings section that details the essential outcomes of your investigation; and
4. Discussion section that explains and evaluates your findings in the context of existing knowledge.

The introductory section begins with a general overview of your research topic. This becomes increasingly specific as you introduce the research questions you are going to pursue, the methods you will use to do that and then the results that those methods give. The dissertation will then become more general again as you relate your specific findings to the wider context. It is useful to imagine a camera. You start with a wide-angled lens which takes in the surrounding environment. Then you focus in closely using the zoom to look in detail at your subject. Then you zoom out again to see the bigger picture. A typical dissertation format is as detailed in Figure 1.2.

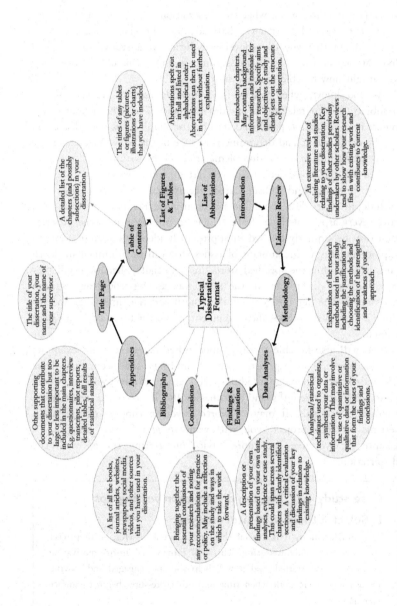

Figure 1.2 A typical dissertation format and contents structure

Table of Contents
A detailed list of the chapters (and possibly subsections) in your dissertation.

List of Figures & Tables
The titles of any tables or figures (pictures, illustrations or charts) that you have included.

List of Abbreviations
Abbreviations spelt out in full and listed in alphabetical order. Abbreviations can then be used in the text without further explanation.

Introduction
Introductory chapters. May contain background information and rationale for your research. Specify aims and objectives of study and clearly sets out the structure of your dissertation.

Literature Review
An extensive review of existing literature and studies relating to your dissertation. Key findings of other studies previously undertaken by other scholars. Reviews tend to show how your research fits in with existing work and contributes to current knowledge.

Methodology
Explanation of the research methods used in your study including the justification for choosing the methods and identification of the strengths and weakness of your approach.

Data Analyses
Analytical/statistical techniques used to organise, synthesis your data or information. This may involve the use of quantitative or qualitative data or information that form the bases of your findings and conclusions.

Findings & Evaluation
A description or presentation of your own data, findings based on your own data, analyses, evidence or case study. This could span across several chapters with clearly identified sections. A critical evaluation and discussion of your key findings in relation to existing knowledge.

Conclusions
Bringing together the essential conclusions of your research and noting any recommendations for practice or policy. May include a reflection on the study and ways in which to take the work forward.

Bibliography
A list of all the books, journal articles, websites, newspapers, social media, videos, and other sources that you have used in your dissertation.

Appendices
Other supporting documents that contribute to your dissertation but too large or less important to be included in the main chapters. E.g. questionnaires, interview transcripts, pilot reports, detailed tables, full results of statistical analysis.

Title Page
The title of your dissertation, your name and the name of your supervisor.

Typical Dissertation Format

Preparing for the dissertation

In certain essential ways, what the dissertation reflects is a direct development from the skills that you have acquired through your programme. If you doubt that you have developed during your study, go back and look at one of your first-year assignments and think of improvements you might now be able to make to it.

As you know, when you write a module assessment, you discuss a subject area in relation to an idea or topic. The title of your essay, report or examination paper and its first paragraph focus your discussion on the chosen topic and determine the scope of the essay. You undertake a careful reading of a selection of material. Then, within the limits prescribed by the assessment title, you attempt to construct a coherent, closely reasoned and substantiated argument. Your essay does not include all your ideas about the literature area, nor does it attempt to cover every aspect of them. Rather, it is an interpretation. The dissertation may be similarly focused in approach. It identifies a single topic to explore and limits the amount of issues that can be examined in depth and detail within the specified word limit. Initially, then, you will prepare for your dissertation in the same way as you would any written assessment. The key difference is the length and the time taken to produce a sustained and justified argument around a topic that you have chosen.

You will also be able to draw upon other experiences, for example, in the analysis and presentation of findings that you may have covered on methodology modules. You are probably aware of where your academic strengths and weaknesses lie. If you have never really thought about this, it may be worth devoting time to doing so. In setting up your project, you will want to *play to your strengths*. In Chapter 3, we give you more advice on getting started with the dissertation.

Case study 1.1 Top ten dissertation writing tips

1. Select a topic that interests you

First and foremost, it is crucial that you select a dissertation or project topic that you find interesting. This will provide the initial motivation you need to get started, and it will help you stay engaged and moving forward with your work when time and other pressures begin to surface later on.

2. Know your topic

You should be absolutely clear in your own mind as to what your dissertation or project topic is. Write this down in a couple of sentences and stick it onto your computer. This will help you to know exactly what you need to do and also help prevent you from getting bogged down in material that is irrelevant.

3. Work with your supervisor

Your supervisor is there to provide guidance to enable you to conduct independent research and write your dissertation according to the conventions and expectations of your particular discipline. However, for most students this will be the first experience of working with a lecturer in such a sustained and focused way. It is important that you know what you can expect from your supervisor from the beginning. And it is equally important for you to know what your supervisor expects of you!

4. Seek peer support

Self-organised writing groups with other students can provide a valuable source of support during what is a particularly demanding and sometimes isolating experience of writing at university. Try meeting regularly with a group of peers to discuss your work and any challenges you are facing.

5. Familiarise yourself with the assessment criteria

It is a good idea to find out early what your tutors will be looking for in your dissertation by getting a copy of the assessment criteria and any other guidance provided.

6. Consider the ethical dimension

If your dissertation involves collecting data from human participants, which is most likely to be the case in the sciences or social sciences, you will need to follow your university's ethical guidelines for such work. You are advised to begin considering the ethical dimension of your work as early as possible.

7. Make good use of subject librarians

Subject librarians are an often overlooked but very valuable resource when it comes to dissertation writing. They have specific knowledge of the journals, books and other resources – both printed and online versions – relevant to your particular discipline.

8. Keep track of your sources

From the very beginning of your literature review, it is important you come up with a simple system for keeping track of the complete bibliographic details of what you read. It is especially important to record specific page numbers for any direct quotations you write down when taking notes.

9. Start writing

What can you do when you don't know what or how to start writing? Start writing! One of the best ways to overcome that hurdle of getting started is to give yourself licence to 'freewrite', to simply write down anything that comes to mind on your topic, without stopping, for ten or fifteen minutes. Don't worry about correct spelling or grammar or even writing in complete sentences as freewriting is a creative process.

10. Stay focused

A dissertation is likely to be the longest piece of writing you will complete as an undergraduate, and the risk of straying away from your topic as you progress with your work is much greater than it is with shorter pieces of writing.

(Harrington et al (2007), Write Now CETL)

Key messages

- The dissertation is an independent piece of research where you are responsible for your own learning.
- It will demand the use of your communication, information-seeking and intellectual skills.
- The social science-based dissertation will normally include standard features, including an introduction, a literature review, methodology, findings, conclusion and bibliographic references.
- You can, and should, value your own experiences and strengths as well as secondary resources.

Key questions

- Do you know and understand the purpose of your dissertation and have you received all the information about the requirements of your dissertation?
- Do you have a working title for your dissertation and the specific research questions you want to answer?

Further reading

Cottrell, S. (2014). *Dissertations and Project Reports: A Step by Step Guide*. Basingstoke: Palgrave Macmillan.

Day, T. (2018). *Success in Academic Writing*, Palgrave Study Skills. London: Palgrave Macmillan.

Dawson, C. (2019). *Introduction to Research Methods 4th Edition*. Oxford: How to Books.

O'Leary, Z. (2018). *Little Quick Fix: Research Proposal*. London: Sage.

Murray, R. (2017). *How to Write a Thesis*. Maidenhead: Open University Press.

Chapter 2

Getting support

Introduction

This chapter explores how you can get support and help with producing your dissertation. It focuses mainly on how your dissertation supervisor (your institution may use a different name such as 'adviser' or 'tutor') can support you and your project and how you can make best use of their feedback. The chapter also considers other forms of support you could actively seek out, including that provided by staff in your library, peer and group support. By the end of this chapter, you should have a better understanding of the following:

- The role of the supervisor
- Your role in the relationship and ideas about becoming an autonomous learner
- How to make the best use of feedback from your supervisor
- Other forms of support that may help you on your dissertation journey.

What is the role of your supervisor?

Although there are many ways to supervise a dissertation, there are some general things that can be said about the supervision process and the relationship between the student and the supervisor. This relationship is one which many institutions see as vital in helping students produce their dissertation. Supervisors:

- Offer guidance as to the best possible way of formulating and carrying out a successful project, based on their experience and aptitude for the role;

- Can provide a lifeline and serve as a calming influence when your dissertation appears too vast to comprehend and to undertake successfully;
- May adopt a variety of roles throughout the dissertation process. At times they will appear to be at the centre of what you are doing, guiding and advising you.

At other times, supervisors will be in the background, there to 'catch you' if needed; they are a resource that you can and should access as you prepare to make the leap to becoming a researcher. Try thinking of supervisors as being like the mirrors in your car: it is worth consulting them before performing any major manoeuvres! Our research (Todd et al. 2004, 2006) shows that students experience different types of supervision and help in the early stages of their dissertations. Students talk about the value of:

- Discussion of general ideas in the early meetings with their supervisor
- Help to make the dissertation more manageable and realistic in its remit
- Help with sharpening the focus
- Help with devising a concise question
- Help with what should be avoided.

How can your supervisor help you to identify and define your research question?

When supervisors first meet their students, they are presented often with ambitious proposals and ideas for dissertations that resemble the kind of work expected at postgraduate level, which are not feasible at undergraduate level. One of the first things, therefore, that a dissertation supervisor will do is support you to establish the limits for your work. Once these limits have been identified, the process of planning and producing a dissertation becomes far less daunting.

It is not the supervisor's responsibility to provide the student with a question but to listen to what you as a student have to say and to help you to devise a suitable question. Supervisors will clearly be influenced by their own experience and expertise, but you can and should expect your supervisor to listen to your ideas and to suggest some ways to make it possible for you to fulfil your aims. Supervisors will often be helpful in providing guidance on sources. Students have noted that the following are particularly useful:

- Reading lists with specific references
- Feedback on the suitability of references they have found
- Reference to general texts that can serve as a starting point.

Your supervisor can have a particularly important role in the early stages of your dissertation, when you start to formulate your ideas and look for some guidance on the possible shape and form of your dissertation.

If you are struggling to come up with proposals for your dissertation or are finding the process overwhelming, making an appointment with your tutor or supervisor enables you to outline your position and to ask for advice (Walliman 2013). As most undergraduate students will have had little experience of formulating their own research questions, supervisors can help determine the scope of the dissertation and make it more manageable. It is important that the questions are answerable. A poorly formulated question can result in the researcher spending unnecessary time struggling to find an answer to something that cannot be answered.

Be upfront and honest about your intentions and aims. To unlock the higher grades you'll need to be keen and really dig in. Your supervisor will only be too happy to help.

What else can you expect from your supervisor?

On a more practical level, students can utilise supervisor support in order to discuss and fully understand the main assessment requirements of the dissertation in terms of:

- The title of the dissertation is and whether it matches what you have actually done
- Presentation (how it looks)
- Organisation (chapters, headed sections)
- Length (not too long or too short)
- List of contents (for navigation)
- Use of abstract (to summarise the dissertation)
- Reference list (to demonstrate background reading).

(Todd et al. 2004; Walliman 2013)

Walliman (2013) stresses the importance of knowing and understanding the requirements of the dissertation and what examiners look for when they allocate marks, particularly if students wish to receive the best possible grade. With the subject and title of the dissertation agreed, you can take the next steps in the dissertation process.

Make regular appointments to see your supervisor. Bear in mind the limited number of student-supervisor meetings, so ensure you make the most of them.

Dissertation supervision can take different forms according to the supervisor's personal approach. This includes whether supervisors insist on regular meetings with their students or operate on a more informal basis that allows students to ask for support when they consider it necessary. However, the majority of students sampled in our research (Todd et al. 2004) had, throughout the course of their dissertation, engaged in some kind of formal arrangement with their supervisor. The majority of these students saw the benefits in this, particularly the help they received in setting tasks and deadlines that served to provide additional motivation and a structure throughout the dissertation process that allowed students to manage their workload more effectively.

See your dissertation supervisor as soon as you have been assigned one and when you have a basic understanding of what you want your dissertation content to be about. Set yourself a timeline and targets to organise your workload, and to aid progress and motivation. Always make sure prior to seeing your supervisor that you have completed the goals set at the previous meeting and what you want from the next meeting.

Reaching agreement with your supervisor

It is important that you and the supervisor are clear about each other's roles in this process. When researching and writing up your dissertation within higher education, it is expected that you will be operating as an autonomous learner. This means that you:

- Take increasing responsibility for your own learning
- Plan a work schedule for yourself and manage your time effectively, using interim deadlines as appropriate
- Devise your own research question(s)
- Employ the research skills you have developed during your degree studies to date
- Negotiate and agree your work plan with your dissertation supervisor
- Pursue your work with rigour and enthusiasm
- Embrace debate with your supervisor.

It is also important that you agree with your supervisor what the appropriate type of support is. Dissertations will certainly vary in complexity. The more complex methodology you employ, the more guidance you will need. In general, a dissertation that seeks to analyse a range of theoretical sources will be easier to organise than one which relies upon drafting questionnaires, running focus groups and arranging a series of interviews. Walliman (2013) suggests that students should:

- Be sure to ask what arrangements are in place for meetings with their supervisor (e.g. whether these are organised on a weekly basis or particular slots booked in advance);
- Recognise that dissertation supervisors expect students attend meetings with something to discuss, whether these are ideas or written work;
- be punctual for pre-arranged meetings as a common courtesy;
- make sure to notify supervisors if you cannot make pre-arranged meetings;
- reach an agreement on the organisation of meetings and the form these meetings take – if you find that the method used does not suit your learning style, then address this as early as possible and renegotiate the form that the supervision meetings take.

Group supervision

As said earlier, the most common practice is one-to-one meetings with your supervisor. It is sometimes useful to have supervision meetings in groups, however. This allows the supervisor to provide some general advice on a range of issues, particularly at the early stages, and this can be very valuable for sharing common issues and questions, for hearing the ideas of others to help you reflect on your own and generally to know you are not alone in managing a complex task!

Email and virtual meetings

Supervisors might also suggest email correspondence. This can be particularly useful when you want to address specific questions. However, be aware that email can be torrential for many academic staff, and students need to appreciate the many demands on their supervisor's time!

Email is particularly useful to ask succinct, specific questions about references or methodology. Email can be used to send your draft chapters to your supervisor and to deal with smaller issues between supervision sessions. Emails can help with immediate response to issues, if the supervisor is available. This avoids the problem of having to wait for a meeting, and it is often the case that specific information is easy to communicate by email. Emails are less helpful when you want to discuss ideas and work towards a solution, so it is often better to arrange to see your supervisor for these, or a Skype/FaceTime meeting may be more feasible.

Feedback on draft chapters

An important part of the supervision process consists of the supervisor's feedback. The approach to feedback will vary between institutions, but supervisors will usually provide at least some feedback on your written work. We recommend you get feedback from your supervisor on the first draft of the dissertation proposal and introductory chapters (or any other of the dissertation chapters). While you should take the comments of your supervisor on board, and the option this gives you to change your work, Walliman (2013) suggests that it is important to think through such alterations and their implications before doing so. Supervisors provide feedback for guidance only. Your supervisor will advise you to do certain things to make your work clearer or to elevate its analytical qualities. You may disagree with their advice. You take responsibility for your work so may disregard their comments.

We would recommend you take full advantage of all the supervision time available to you. Even if you think you have made very little progress between meetings, that contact with someone and the opportunity for discussion is invaluable. It's entirely possible that your best ideas might only make themselves apparent to you when you try to explain your thoughts to someone else, and obviously your supervisor's experience as a researcher puts him or her in the best possible place to support you.

Remember also that your dissertation is unique, and supervisors are simply giving you the best advice that they can based upon their own experience and their own academic expertise. It is worth paying particular attention, however, to advice on structural issues. Such advice is often of value regardless of the subject matter of your dissertation. It is worth noting that a dissertation that ignores academic conventions and does not make sense to your supervisor is unlikely to attract a high mark.

As your knowledge of your chosen dissertation topic is not supposed to be absolute – hence one of the main reasons for doing a dissertation – supervisors will be able to tell you whether you have missed any important theories or theorists from the review of literature. Supervisors can also help with practical issues such as the writing style adopted in the dissertation (formal or informal) and the required length of not only the overall dissertation but also each of the individual chapters so that the dissertation achieves a balance (Walliman 2013).

It is important to develop a relationship in which you feel comfortable with engaging in an ongoing critical dialogue related to your work so that you value the comments and ideas offered. Supervisors have a vested interest in bringing out the best in your work. They will have to read and evaluate your work and often will have to argue its merits with a second marker and even with external examiners. The clearer you can make it, the better it will be received by all concerned.

Why is supervision so important? Can't you just get on with your dissertation on your own?

From what has been said already, it should be clearer that the supervision process is an important part of researching and writing your dissertation. While some students will not take advantage of the supervision offered by their institutions, evidence from our research (Todd et al. 2004) suggests that students who choose to pursue their dissertation without consulting their supervisor often find it difficult to maintain momentum and are apt to make fundamental errors in the way they approach their work. Many students, however, recognise that their supervisors have an important role to play and value their encouragement, guidance and reassurance on their direction, without taking control of their dissertations and telling them what to do.

Good supervisors should:

- Set clear boundaries and expectations at the beginning of the supervision process;
- Inform you of their availability;
- Be honest about their own research strengths and limitations;
- Listen;
- Help you reflect on what you are doing and why;
- Work in partnership with you;
- Provide strategies to enable you to solve your own problems;
- Ask questions, not tell you what to do, and expect you to have questions for them;
- Not impose their ideas on you;
- Share their own research experiences in a way that illuminates issues for you;
- Challenge you to succeed.

(Kandlbinder and Peseta 2006)

Managing difficulties with supervisors

It is important that you find ways to negotiate your learning with your supervisor. Robson (2014) points out that supervisors will have their own preconceptions about what constitutes a successful project. While it is natural for students to follow the advice given, different approaches should not be ruled out if students can put forward a suitable argument for doing so and a good supervisor should be receptive to these.

If you have serious concerns about the level and type of support you are receiving, Robson (2014) suggests that there should be avenues for redressing this problem.

In terms of access to your supervisor he also urges students to be reasonable and to acknowledge that supervisors have busy schedules. You need to be clear of your own role within the dissertation process. At the end of the day, it remains the case that the dissertation is the responsibility of the student. Although supervisors can provide guidance, it is not their responsibility to write the dissertation for their students.

Once you are allocated to a supervisor by your university, it is not normally possible to change this arrangement. On rare occasions, however, you may find that you cannot work with the allocated supervisor. In the first instance, you should try to discuss the difficulties with the supervisor and attempt to resolve these through some agreed action plan. If you do not find it easy to do this face-to-face, write down your concerns in an email; this allows you to be clear about the issues (perhaps ask a friend to read it before sending it to check the tone and that the meaning is clear). If, after this, it becomes evident that the relationship has broken down irrevocably, you should contact the dissertation tutor, or whoever is responsible for the module, directly to discuss other possible arrangements. It is important to sort out such difficulties as soon as possible.

Dissertation support and information technologies

The social sciences are, by their very nature, influenced and shaped by social trends. The use of technologies in conducting investigation and undertaking academic study has become a common phenomenon, especially amongst students and the younger generation of academics. Social media plays an important role in this development. Throughout this book, we indicate where information technologies and social media may be deployed effectively in your dissertation, for example in finding resources, conducting data collection, disseminating the findings of your research, and networking with other researchers.

We live in an information-driven society with a multitude of data about our social world being generated every day through strings of aural and visual images and texts produced by increasingly sophisticated technology. More than at any time in human history, there is easy and growing access to mass communications through different media and various platforms. In addition to the traditional old media such as film, magazines, newspapers, radio and TV we now have a multitude of new media such as the internet, world wide web, social media, digital TV, video on demand, phones, tablets, 'phablets' and other web-based technology with enormous capacity to enable interactions and communications between large numbers of people in a diverse range of settings.

The rapid growth in the sophistication and diversity of communication media has led to the creation of what is now termed the 'information society'. Brought about by the liberalisation of telecommunications and exponential increase in the use of the Internet, 'information society' is a term used to reflect the interacting influence of both information and communication technologies (ICTs). These new technologies have enormous influence on and implications for all aspects of our society and economy, including how you might approach your dissertation.

In this section, we focus specifically on how information technologies and social media can provide a valuable source of information to you in terms of what you can access, but also huge opportunities for peer discussion groups and networking. It is also a platform to share research ideas, worries and strategies about your dissertation.

There are numerous online discussion forums that you can join that you may find useful for your research. For the social sciences, see www.socialpsychology.org/forums.htm and www.thestudentroom.co.uk for all subject interests.

You may benefit from sharing your dissertation ideas with other learners from a wide range of backgrounds and institutions around the world as you are able to network with other people through these media. We discuss some of those platforms below. The ability to interact with other students and to share ideas in a safe online environment can help build a network of support that you may find useful in writing your dissertation. ICTs also provide an effective new way of gathering primary data or sourcing secondary data, as is shown in Chapters 6 and 7.

Table 2.1 Selected social media and new information technologies and possible usage in dissertations

Social media/new technologies	Main purpose	Possible usage
Facebook	Social networking	• Networking with other researchers • Communicating with and receiving information and support from others for your dissertation • Collecting data, e.g. online questionnaire administration • Linking with academic events, posts and discussions
Twitter	Online microblogging	• Getting snap information or ideas for your dissertation • Following other people's 'tweets' • Staying informed about current affairs, events and issues • Broadcasting snaps of your research findings
WhatsApp	Messaging app	• Staying in touch with people, other students and friends • Sending and receiving text messages, voice calls, video calls, photos and documents
Instagram	Social networking	• Sharing photos and videos • Following your friends • Engaging and connecting with people interested in your dissertation
Blogs	Discussion or information website	• Sharing ideas, photos and videos • Collecting data, e.g. pasting/asking questions on blogs • Following current discussions • Gather information or ideas from other bloggers • Feedback from other researchers
Google+	Social networking	• Networking with other people • Sharing information about your dissertation with others
Wikipedia	Online open contents	• Creating and publishing articles about your dissertation • Editing other contents and materials created by other people

(*Continued*)

Table 2.1 (Cont.)

Social media/new technologies	Main purpose	Possible usage
LinkedIn	Social networking	• Creating and managing your professional identity • Networking with other people in your profession • Documenting people you know or trust professionally • Messaging and sharing contacts
Dropbox	Cloud file hosting and storage	• Storing your data • Sharing your files – text, photos, videos etc. • Sending and previewing Dropbox files
OneDrive	Cloud file storage	• Storing and sharing files and photos, documents etc. • Synchronising documents in your local computer with documents stored in the cloud, preventing loss of data • Safeguarding your dissertation data nd documents
Foursquare	Local search and discovery app	• Searching events' location or things based on your Internet browsing history • Locating places and social networking
Reddit	Social news website	• Following current discussions on specific issues relating to your dissertation • Creating stories about your dissertation for others to read and comment or vote upon • Following thread discussion on specific topic of interest to you • Monitor how your content is rated by other users
Tumblr	Microblogging and social networking	• Creating a blog around your dissertation • Connect with and follow the blogs of other Tumblr users
Pinterest	Visual social website	• Finding images online and their source • Checking the original source of images • Organising/categorising images relating to your dissertation.

Social networking platforms

Social media is the general term used to refer to the collection of online communications channels that are designed for people to contribute to and share contents, and interact with a large number of people through collaboration and sharing of ideas. These community-based arrangements of generating and sharing information are organised via different platforms.

Social networking can also offer some other educational benefits and constitute an important aspect of your learning. There are many online courses that you can join to develop your learning further in specific areas relating to your research. Learning with others by forming a peer study group is a great way of motivating yourself. Whether online or offline, meeting and sharing ideas about your dissertation could open up opportunities and make the dissertation experience less lonely and laborious. Knowledge shared is knowledge gained. The more you are able to share ideas with others, the more you are likely to learn about what other people are doing, thereby, gaining new knowledge. In the following section, we provide a brief summary of different social network platforms and how they might help you in your dissertation writing, and some of these are discussed in later chapters.

Facebook – a social networking media site that allows users to share information such as photos, videos and texts. It is also a popular medium for instant messaging and for keeping in touch with people, hosting and publicising social events. You can use this to communicate with other dissertation students, or to collect data from your network of friends.

Twitter – an online microblogging service that allows users to post short messages known as 'tweets'. Tweets are restricted to a maximum of 280 characters and are intended for users to communicate with other users and follow their tweets using different devices and platforms.

WhatsApp – a free messaging app that can be used on smartphones, tablets and other devices. It allows users to send and receive text messages, voice calls, video calls, photos and documents.

Instagram – a photo- and video-sharing social network, owned by Facebook, Inc. Instagram allows users to engage and connect with other people. It is a simplified version of Facebook with a focus on mobile use and visual sharing.

Wikipedia – an online content created through collaboration of users generating materials for public use. The community of users known as

Wikipedians can create content for publication and edit or add to other people's content.

LinkedIn – a social networking site mostly used by the business community to connect with people with similar profession or professional interests and to share resources or information about events. It allows users to create and manage their professional identity.

Reddit – a social news website and forum where users create or promote contents through voting. It is a community of users made up of many sub-groups called 'subreddits' with each subreddit focusing on specific areas of study such as history, politics, music, technology etc. Users get a constantly updating feed of breaking news and conversations on their selected topic or areas of interest and read reviews and compare content ratings of other users.

Pinterest – a visual social website designed for sharing images found online and their original source. It allows people to find information on the internet through images. Users are able to click on an image and are then redirected to the original source.

Dropbox – a file sharing and storage service. It enables users to upload files onto Dropbox servers and make them available for use or download anywhere using your computer or mobile devices.

OneDrive – a Microsoft cloud storage service that allows users to store their documents, files, photos, videos, etc. securely and then access them anywhere. It is a data recovery mechanism that allows users to sync data in their computer with data stored in the cloud, thereby preventing loss of data in case of computer failure.

Foursquare – a local search and discovery app that allows users to find places near them based on their browsing history. It can be used to search for places or things like restaurants, shopping locations, events and entertainment centres in cities around the world.

Tumblr – a microblogging and social networking website that allows its users to post multimedia contents to a short-form blog. Tumblr users can connect with and follow other users and have the option to make their blogs private or public.

YouTube – a free online video-sharing platform with extensive learning content; just make sure you are a critical viewer.

You may find some of these platforms particularly useful in terms of support for your dissertation. Through Twitter, Facebook, Instagram and LinkedIn, you might find a network of like-minded people, where you can share ideas, events and resources, while WhatsApp could be helpful in keeping in touch with your peer group. You might find that the platforms that you use socially are also useful as part of your academic work.

New technological advances, especially in the area of information technology, have made our lives better. Our social world is constantly changing. The way we learn, study and work has changed significantly since the last decade. Adapting to technological changes is an important part of education. Your dissertation success could depend on how well you are able to understand, use and adapt new technologies to achieve your aims. As modern society becomes increasingly defined by technological advances, it is important to embrace the opportunities new information technologies offer. You also need to be mindful of the limitations of new technologies and to deploy them appropriately in your dissertation. In the context of writing your dissertation, new technologies should be considered as tools. They are a means to an end. Therefore, use them effectively to support your study objectives.

Many universities have different policies with regards to information technologies and social networking. While some institutions provide support and guidance on social media use and new technologies, there may be some tools and platforms that your university does not support, or even that you are not allowed to use. Make sure you consult your dissertation supervisor for guidance.

Information technologies and dissertation supervision

While most of your supervision sessions for your dissertation will be individual and with your dissertation supervisor, group supervisions are becoming an important feature of dissertation supervision in many institutions. Group supervisions can be a useful way of achieving additional support and motivation for your project. While this traditionally may have been face-to-face, technologies such as Socrative Student, Socrative Teacher, Nearpod and other Presentation Apps are being increasingly being used to conduct group supervision of undergraduate dissertations. Your supervisor may well be using these or similar Apps in supervising your dissertations. If so, it is important that you are familiar with how these new technologies may be used by your supervisor to support your dissertation (see Case study 2.1).

Much has been written on the use of technology to enhance teaching and students' learning experience, yet specific ways in which technology could be used as a tool for undertaking group dissertation supervision is relatively new.

Case study 2.1 New technology and dissertation supervision: Using 'Socrative Student' and 'Socrative Teacher' apps

This case study shows how a dissertation supervisor uses the Socrative apps to conduct group supervision in an HE institution. It is an example of how new technologies could be effectively used to support group rather than individual student supervision. It involves the use of a free app – Socrative Student – which all the dissertation students were asked to download to their mobile devices such as phones, tablets, phablets, laptops or any Wi-Fi enabled device.

Through a companion free app – Socrative Teacher – the supervisor was able to assess and evaluate students' engagement and progress with their dissertations at different stages of the process.

The objective was to assess students' progress in their dissertation by responding to the following questions or tasks through the app using their devices.

1   What is your dissertation topic/title?
2   What are your main research questions?
3   List five key words to describe your research topic.
4   List the main sources of data/information you've collected for your dissertation.
5   Provide a short description of your research methodology for your dissertation.
6   List two main theories that relate to or underpin your research.
7   What method of analysis are you using in your dissertation and why?
8   What are the main findings, so far, of your research?
9   Briefly explain any policy implications of your main research findings.
10 What are the essential skills acquired in the course of doing your dissertation?
11 Are you satisfied by your progress with your dissertation?
12 Will you be able to submit your dissertation by the deadline?

These questions were pushed directly to students' devices via a quiz room named **Dissertation Room** that was created for the purpose of the exercise, a virtual room in which students could respond anywhere in the world with Internet connection. The students' answers to the questions were automatically recorded live on the **Socrative Teacher** app. Through the students' responses, the supervisor was able to gain an insight into the individual students' progress and engagement with their dissertation regardless of their locations.

Each student's progress was captured and then compared with other dissertation students' progress. Students with specific problem in any of the 12 areas of enquiry were identified and targeted support provided to them. A total of 30 students were involved in this case study.

With this app the supervisor has a real-time snapshot of the students' progress on their dissertation. Using this technology allows supervisors to identify specific areas of support for their dissertation students. It is a cost effective and time-saving method of assessing students' work and offers a more consistent, reliable way of monitoring students' progress.

Who else may be able to help you?

Producing a dissertation can be an isolating task, one in which you find the nature of the work and study timetable reduces opportunities for mixing with other students. You may be someone who is comfortable working alone, or you may be the type of learner who is motivated and energised by a more social learning environment. In this section, we consider other people who may be able to help you navigate your way through the dissertation journey successfully and who may also be able to reduce a sense of isolation if you are experiencing this. In the previous section on changing supervisors we gave you a modest example of how you might ask a friend for support. You may wish to think about who else may have expertise or qualities that you could draw support from.

Library and other institutional support services

Library staff have a wealth of expertise in research approaches and can direct you to useful databases and reference material. In many institutions, the library staff will offer specific workshops or one-to-one support for students undertaking dissertation research.

The range of written and in-person support has been a positive consequence of the expansion of higher education and growth in student numbers. Most institutions now provide comprehensive guidance on a wide range of study-skills support. These may be available through libraries or other central support units or within faculties and departments. At the start of your dissertation, you may find it helpful to access and read relevant guidance on, for example:

- Writing styles
- Referencing
- Searching
- Time management.

You may have been given such documents at the start of your programme and they are now buried at the bottom of a pile of papers. Now is the time to dig them out and use them. In addition to investing in provision of written support materials, there are usually individual staff with a remit to help with specific areas of student support, particularly those with specific learning needs associated with, for example, dyslexia or having a first language other than the one they are learning in.

Other academic staff

It is common for supervisors to be assigned students who choose a topic that is not within their area of specialism. This does not have to impact on the quality of support you receive, but you might wish to consult with other academic staff in your department or other institutions for ideas on your topic, for example, with key reading. This is reasonable but be aware that they may be very busy so do not feel offended if they are not able to respond to you within your preferred timescales. If you do want to ask something, keep your request short, simple and reasonable.

Administrative staff

Administrative staff are the backbone in institutions and will often be the best people to consult if you have practical questions about deadlines, requirements for binding, etc. If you have questions that you think they could answer then try them before your supervisor: the response may be quicker.

Other students

Dissertation writing groups are often developed to support graduate students with writing their dissertations, but they are also useful for undergraduate studies. Such groups might meet regularly but are informal in nature. Your university or college may have a procedure for the establishment of such groups, or you could set an informal group up yourself. For them to work successfully it is important that group rules and expectations are established and maintained. Such groups could operate in a face-to-face or virtual environment. The benefits may include:

- Reducing isolation
- Motivation to stick to project timelines
- Critical friends with whom to discuss specific ideas, challenges and 'knotty problems'
- Sounding issues out in advance of meeting a supervisor
- Putting things in perspective if you are feeling stressed or under pressure
- Sharing resources and search results.

Such benefits can be gained through one-to-one peer or pair support with like-minded fellow students(s). You may also wish to search for support on the internet in regard to 'dissertation writing groups' which could provide you an additional support structure to navigate through the dissertation writing process. In addition to offering you readily accessible support and feedback, these groups can also make you feel less isolated and you soon realise you are not the only person undertaking the 'big kahuna' – the writing of a dissertation. Try doing a search for dissertation writing groups and see what you come up with. You might want to start with Phinished (www.phinished.org/). This is a forum aimed primarily at postgraduate students (Masters and Doctorates) who are struggling to finish writing their dissertations and theses. As an undergraduate student, you still might find some useful advice and guidance about the different parts of your dissertation.

As discussed above, social networking platforms such as Twitter and Instagram can also provide a useful forum for sharing and discussing ideas and progress.

Work-based supervisors, colleagues and users of services

If you are working and studying or on a course such as social work, involving access to a work environment that is related to your subject of study, and many social science students will be as part of a placement, internship, through voluntary or paid work, you may be able to discuss ideas and seek guidance or feedback from supervisors and colleagues there. If you are undertaking an applied or practice-focused dissertation, this will be invaluable. You may also wish to consult with staff from other agencies who you have identified as being particularly experienced or expert in an area related to your topic.

Friends and family

There are all sorts of ways in which friends and family may provide emotional and practical support – from making you cups of coffee to reading and proofreading extracts of content. We all want to achieve a good study/home/work to life balance, and each of us has our own way of finding our way through this, but we recognise this is not easy!

Key messages

* Initially, ask your supervisor for advice on your choice of topic and your reading.
* Talk to your supervisor, preferably at regular meetings, the frequency of which should be agreed upon mutually.
* If this is allowed in your department, show draft chapters to your supervisor as soon as you have them: give your supervisor time to read, think and give feedback.
* Your supervisor will offer constructive criticisms of your work: that is why he or she is there. It is not a criticism of you, or of your ability. Do not be shy or embarrassed by this.
* Your personal supervisor is a resource: use that resource to your advantage. Ask them questions: about methodology, theory or anything else that may occur. You are not expected to be an instant expert – that's their job!
* Your supervisor will help you but not do your work for you. Supervisors can only work with what you bring them.
* Your supervisor may choose to use new technology to carry out supervision of your dissertation.
* Social media provides great opportunity to connect and share ideas with other people.
* Try to draw a network of other support around you to reduce any sense of isolation and to increase access to useful expertise and help – both on and off campus. Information technologies and social networking platforms may be useful here.

Key questions

- Are you clear about the role of your supervisor and how he or she can support you and your work?
- Are you making the most of the objectivity and honesty the supervisor can offer to help you improve your work?
- Do you prepare for meetings to make the most of the time you have available?
- Are you keeping in touch throughout the work process?
- Who else can support you with your work and how?

Further reading

Bell, J. and Waters, S. (2018). *Doing Your Research Project: A Guide for First Time Researchers* (7th Edition). London: Oxford University Press.

Greetham, B. (2014). *How to Write Your Undergraduate Dissertation*. 2nd Edition). London: Palgrave Macmillan.

Robson, C. (2014). *How to Do a Research Project: A Guide for Undergraduate Students*. 2nd Edition). Chichester: Wiley.

Todd, M., Bannister, P. and Clegg, S. (2004). Independent Inquiry and the Undergraduate Dissertation: Perceptions and Experiences of Final-Year Social Science Students. *Assessment and Evaluation in Higher Education*, 29 (3), 335–355.

Walliman, N. (2013) *Your Undergraduate Dissertation: The Essential Guide for Success*. London: Sage.

Chapter 3

Research questions and getting started on your dissertation

Introduction

This chapter explains how to start with your dissertation by posing the right questions. Most dissertations that fail do so because they set out by asking the wrong questions. This chapter will help you formulate the essential questions to successfully initiate your social research project. It will guide you on strategies for planning your dissertation and offer advice on the most effective way to start your investigation.

Often the dissertation involves many months of work, and it is important that you manage your time effectively and be well organised. Unsurprisingly, because of competing demands on time, many students do not always devise and follow a structured work schedule, which can have implications for the quality of work produced, not to mention stress levels!

By the end of this chapter, you should have a better understanding of:

- How to best prepare for a dissertation
- How to find a dissertation topic
- How to refine that topic into a workable research question
- How to plan to manage and complete all the work required before your dissertation deadline.

Deciding on study objectives and preparing for a dissertation

The first stage in preparing a dissertation is deciding the main purpose of your research and what you want to achieve in terms of objectives.

Figure 3.1 Key research objectives of dissertation

The main research objectives of doing dissertation are summarised below and shown in Figure 3.1.

A dissertation may have any one or a combination of the below listed objectives.

1. **Describing** social events, situations or phenomena with the purpose of establishing any underlying structure. Describing things can sometimes tell us whether an observed phenomenon is what is ideal or expected and how what we observed can help us predict future events if the same situation occurs in the future.

2. **Explaining** simple or complex issues through a deeper investigation into their underlying processes. The main purpose here may be to dig deeper into why and how things happen and making sense of various factors or variables that may contribute to our understanding of social issues. This also provides the opportunity to explore the complex social, economic, political, cultural, environmental, and other factors relating to the events or issues we seek to explain.

3. **Evaluating** or making informed judgements about the nature, quality, characteristics or impact of social events or objects. The main purpose here could be to assess the effectiveness of a social policy,

government programmes, development strategies, etc., with a view of measuring their impact on society.

4. **Comparing** things, events or ideas in order to highlight differences and similarities between them. The main purpose of a comparative study may be to seek to understand how, why and to what degree things are similar or different. To fully understand social events, we often need to be able to tell the difference between things. Our understanding of difference also helps form our sense of unity, leading to a better understanding of social phenomena. The basis of comparison could be based on events' characteristics, time, place, intensity and many other considerations depending on the research aims and objectives.

5. **Correlating** two or more events or variables in order to establish any connections between phenomena or variables. The main purpose of correlation studies could be to explore any apparent or hidden relationships between things to help us determine if and how one variable influences the other. Study of relationships could confirm any obvious or hidden interconnections between things and how variables interact and influence each other. The measures of association involved in many correlation studies enable us to make judgements on the strength and direction of connection between different events or variables.

6. **Predicting** social behaviour, phenomena or events, in order to speculate on any future events or trends based on what we already know. Once the strengths and direction of relationships between two or more variables have been established, it is possible to forecast what future trends and relationships are likely to be, all things being equal. The research purpose here could be establishing how to use our knowledge of what we know now about the social world to predict what is likely to happen in the future under similar circumstances.

7. **Controlling** events or social phenomena based on our understanding of the connections between variables and our ability to predict the behaviour of social, economic, environmental or political systems. An effective control demands that we understand any causal relationships that exist between things and knowledge of how one variable affects the other. The main purpose, in a control study, is to seek to manage the effect or impact of social policy on a section of society.

As explained in Chapter 1, a dissertation is a piece of assessment that provides you with a unique opportunity to explore in depth a subject in which you have a personal interest or to further develop an interest from previous study. It may also be that you want to choose a topic related to a career aspiration. Researching and writing a dissertation is hard work, but it should also be rewarding. Remember, your dissertation could make a difference to your field of enquiry.

Some of the first stages of your dissertation are quite like deciding where to go on holiday. There are many factors that may influence your choice: will you choose a trekking holiday in the Andes or a beach holiday on the Mediterranean or camping in Cornwall? There will be factors that influence your decision, such as: what resources do you have available; who are you going with; how much time do you have; what do you enjoy doing?

Selecting a topic for your dissertation, like choosing where to go on holiday, is not always easy and can require a lot of thought. Some people are fortunate: an idea for a dissertation may pop into their mind immediately. Others may have always been interested in an area of investigation and want to do more in-depth research into it. For many, however, this is not the case, and you may need to be more systematic in your search for *the* dissertation question or topic that you wish to explore further.

In any case, it is good practice to do a great deal of thinking and background reading before you reach a final decision about the topic in which you want to invest a lot of time and effort (just as you wouldn't spend a lot of money on a holiday without taking a bit of time exploring options). Your dissertation supervisor could be crucial in helping you decide your topic – so don't be afraid to ask for advice.

Finding a topic for the dissertation

If you are struggling to determine your dissertation topic there are several things that you can do to stimulate thoughts:

- Talk to members of academic staff and other students in your department (either directly or in an online discussion forum) at an early stage about your ideas.
- Make up a list of unresolved questions and issues you had from other courses and modules that you have studied. You could use the reading and knowledge from these to develop a dissertation question.
- Read the news and other media to identify topical issues related to areas of social policy, politics, sociology, criminology, international relations, current/world affairs, etc.

- Draw upon your own experience (as an employee, a parent, part of a campaigning group, a student, a patient and so on) and use this experience to help you define your topic area.
- Think about a book you found interesting or scan through academic journals to find areas that capture your interest and your imagination. Are there any key writers who have shaped your interest or whose views conflict with yours?

Clarifying ideas and narrowing focus

So, let's assume that you now have several potential topic areas in mind. In fact, you may feel you now have too much choice and don't know which area to focus upon! The following checklist may be helpful in deciding which topic to develop into your dissertation research question:

- Can the topic you have selected be addressed in an appropriately academic manner?
- Can the topic be fully explored within the time frame you have for this module (noting that you will have commitments to other modules as well as other non-academic commitments)?
- What are the resource constraints of the dissertation? For example, you may be interested in exploring the views of Scottish members of parliament on the issue of Scottish independence, but if you are based in Exeter how feasible is this in terms of travel time and costs?
- Following on from this, will your question determine the research methods you should employ? Using the above illustration of Scottish members of parliament for example could be explored using a desk-based approach, a postal questionnaire, focus groups or one to one interviews.
- Will the topic be able to sustain your interest over the months to come?

In summary, when you have identified an area that you would like to pursue further, you need to assess whether your topic can be researched within the time you have available and within the resources that you have available. Remember that you should avoid too broad a topic or one that is overly ambitious: it is better to find a thoroughly researched and argued answer to a small question than to fail to find the answer to one which is too big or diffuse.

Try to choose a topic that will sustain your interest. This may be:

- An area of social life that appeals to you
- A type of method that you would like to use
- A body of facts, a theory or concept that you are interested in exploring.

Bringing all three of these together is a way of narrowing the focus of the dissertation into a manageable project. Always keep in mind that your dissertation (although possibly 10,000 words), in reality is an extremely small research project: so at every turn you should be narrowing the focus, not expanding it. A good piece of well-argued and focused research will get a far better mark than a larger incoherent one.

Another way of narrowing the focus is to think about what you are particularly interested in. Write a paragraph that would give someone else a clear picture of the issues. How has your interest developed over time? Can you identify incidents or experiences that have generated your interest? Finally, consider where would you like the work to lead in the longer term and whether this research relates to work you currently do or would like to do at some stage.

In the following case study, Tsang Kwok Kuen, a social science graduate, describes what he felt was important in choosing his dissertation topic.

Case study 3.1   Choosing my dissertation topic

My research topic was on the theme of ingratiation. Why did I choose it? It was because I had observed that many people in Hong Kong seemed to like to flatter others. Why did they do that? I didn't know, so I really wanted to understand this phenomenon deeply. In fact, I tried to study it when I was at secondary school. I took a subject then called Liberal Studies that required me to conduct some research. I chose to study ingratiation. Because of my lack of research skills at that time, I didn't design my research very well and found out nothing. This bad result motivated me to study the same area and topic for my dissertation because I was still curious to find out more about ingratiation.

After deciding on a research area, I started to read literature. I didn't only read the literature related to ingratiation but also read the Chinese Indigenised Social Psychology literature. Actually, I know that some of my friends didn't read much literature.

This was because the literature was too difficult and boring for them. However, I discovered the literature was not as boring as many people thought – maybe the discussions in the literature were related to things I was really interested in. As I kept reading, I got more and more insights into my topic. These insights motivated me to read and think continually. As a result, I formed my own idea about how to write the dissertation.

My experience tells me that doing something you are interested in is very important for you when you are writing a dissertation. Therefore, your interest is an essential source for you to start to think about your own project. For example, one of my friends decided to study the relationship between pets and pet owners. It was because she loved animals and had many pets. If you can find something like this you will enjoy and be motivated to do this difficult piece of work. Look and find a topic from an area you're interested in!

(Tsang Kwok Kuen)

Having identified your topic, you must then develop a question, identifying what you hope to learn. Finding a question sounds as though it will be easier than finding a topic, but, in fact, research questions usually need to be shaped and crafted quite extensively. We will look at this issue in the next section.

What is a good research question?

It is important to start your thinking about the dissertation with a *question* once you have chosen a topic heading. The question sets out what you hope to learn about the topic. This question, together with your approach, will guide and structure the choice of data to be collected and analysed. Some research questions focus your attention onto the relationship of certain theories and concepts, for example, 'How does gender relate to career choices of members of different religions?'

Some research questions aim to open an area to let possible new theories emerge: 'What is going on here?' is the most basic research question in exploratory research. For an undergraduate dissertation, your question needs to be much more targeted than either of these.

Creating a research question is a task. Good research questions are formed, shaped and worked on and are very rarely simply found. You start with what interests you and refine it until it is academically rigorous and workable. There is no recipe for the perfect research question, but there are bad research questions. The following guidelines highlight some of the features of good questions:

- Relevant
- Manageable in terms of research and in terms of your own academic abilities
- Substantial and with original dimensions
- Consistent with the requirements of the assessment
- Clear and simple
- Interesting.

Relevant

The research question you pose should be of academic and intellectual interest to people in your field. The question may arise from issues raised in the literature or in practice. You should be able to establish a clear purpose for your research in relation to the chosen field. For example, are you filling a gap in knowledge, analysing academic assumptions or professional practice, monitoring a development in practice, comparing different approaches or testing theories within a specific population?

Manageable

You need to be realistic about the scope and scale of the project. The question you ask must be within your ability to tackle it. For example:

- Are you able to *access* people, statistics or documents from which you will collect the data you need to address the question fully?
- Are you able to relate the concepts of your research question to the observations, phenomena, indicators or variables you can access?
- Can this data be accessed within the limited *time* and *resources* you have available to you?

Sometimes a research question appears feasible, but when you start your fieldwork or library study, it proves otherwise. In this situation, it is important to write up the problems you have come across honestly and to reflect on what has been learnt. You should also develop a contingency plan to anticipate possible problems of access.

Substantial and (within reason) original

The question should not simply copy questions asked in other final-year modules or modules previously undertaken. The question you devise should show your own social science imagination and your ability to construct and develop research issues. And it needs to give enough scope to develop into a dissertation.

Consistent with the requirements of the assessment

The question must give you the scope to satisfy the learning outcomes of the course. For example, you can choose to conduct a theoretical study, one that does not contain analysis of empirical data. In this case, it will be necessary for you to think carefully before making such a choice. You would be required to give an account of your methodology, to explain why theoretical analysis was the most appropriate way of addressing the question and how you have gone about using theoretical models to produce new insights about the subject. Make sure that you study the requirements of the dissertation and that your research question will fulfil these requirements. Again, if you are still not sure, a discussion with your supervisor or course leader would be helpful here. Check your home institutions' dissertation archive and scan through past dissertations, especially those that were known to have achieved high grades.

Clear and simple

The complexity of a question can frequently hide unclear thoughts and lead to a confused research process. A very elaborate research question, or a question which is not differentiated into different parts, may hide concepts that are contradictory or potentially not relevant at all. Getting this clear and thought through is one of the hardest parts of your work.

Equally, you will want to get started with your literature review and data collection, and you may feel tempted to 'make do' with a broad and vague research question for the moment. However, a muddled question is likely to generate muddled data and equally muddled analysis.

If you create a clear and simple research question, you may find that it becomes more complex as you think about the situation you are studying and undertake the literature review. Having one key question with several sub-components will guide your research here.

Interesting

This is key: the question needs to be one that interests you and is likely to remain intriguing for the duration of the project. There are two traps to be avoided.

First, some questions are *convenient* – the best you can come up with when you are asked to state a question on a form, maybe – or perhaps the question fits in with your units so you decide it will suffice.

Second, some questions are *fads*. They arise out of a set of personal circumstances, for example, a job application. Once the circumstances change you can lose enthusiasm for the topic and it becomes very tedious.

Make sure that you have a real, grounded interest in your research question and that you can explore this and back it up by academic and intellectual debate. It is your interest that will motivate you to keep working and to produce a good dissertation.

As you develop your research question, think carefully about what you would like to find out about. You might have a hypothesis – i.e. a belief about something (founded upon evidence) – which has never been fully tested, proved or disproved. You may, on the other hand, want to couch your interest in terms of an exploration of issues, attitudes or experiences or as a question. Write a list of all the questions you want to answer and group them into priorities or hierarchies and show the connections between them. At this stage, you may want to do some weeding out of overlapping or less relevant questions. It is helpful to list your questions and then to address why you want to know the answer and how it will help you to pursue your overall enquiry.

Taking notes

The process of thinking about the dissertation topic and question is an evolving one. It may help to get some form of personal recording of the ideas, links and resources that you come across in the initial thinking and information-gathering stages. Do not simply rely on your memory to store all the strands of information you come across. A key part of success in dissertation-writing is being organised and systematic in your approach, and the earlier you can adopt this, the better. It is found that keeping a research diary, where you can also record your thoughts, can prove particularly useful. This type of note-taking may link into the writing of other learning logs or personal development planning you are doing already within your degree. Many people find it useful to keep a research notebook in which you can record:

- Questions or ideas that interest you
- Possible ways of researching these
- References to follow up at a later stage
- Sources of information that you have found useful
- Notes on articles and papers you have read or programmes you have seen or heard.

You should keep an accurate record of the bibliographical details of all the material that you read: doing this as you go along will save an enormous amount of time at the end of the project. For more information on literature searching and managing your bibliographical resources, see Chapter 4.

Time-management and work planning

Dissertations usually have a long lead-in time so it is essential that you think about the various stages of work that need to be undertaken and get into good habits early on in the process, for example, keeping records of searches undertaken, ideas that crop up and material to be sought after and incorporated.

You might want to devise a schedule of work from start to finish, or monthly plans, perhaps in discussion with your supervisor or tutor. Nearer the deadline, you may wish to use weekly schedules to keep you on track.

Brainstorming the key research questions, concepts, themes and thoughts will give you some idea of the scale of the task ahead. You may consider producing a timeline to outline the main stages of development in your project.

If you are undertaking empirical work, your planning will need to be even more detailed so that you are aware of slippage that may affect completion of the research.

You will need to allow time for the following activities relating to your study:

- Refining the research question/hypothesis (Chapter 3)
- Checking if your project needs Ethics Committee/School Research Governance approval (Chapter 8)
- Designing the framework for the literature review (Chapter 4)

- Undertaking the literature search and using the framework to develop the review (Chapter 4)
- Developing the methodology for fieldwork and identifying appropriate methods (Chapter 5)
- If required, gaining access and agreeing arrangements for data collection (Chapter 7)
- Collecting the data (Chapter 7)
- Coding or transcribing the data (Chapter 7)
- Analysing data (Chapters 9 and 10)
- Developing the discussion (Chapter 11)
- Writing up the study and conclusions (Chapter 11).

This will all require careful management of time and keeping a check on progress.

You may find it helpful to develop a chart indicating when various stages of work will be undertaken, and with what contingencies. A Gantt chart might work well here. This is a bar-chart-like representation of the work breakdown of your dissertation. It can be made using Microsoft Office Excel to design stacked bar charts. An example of a simple Gantt Chart created to time-manage a dissertation starting at 1 October with the aim of completion by 15 May is shown in Figure 3.2.

Case study 3.2 Procedures for using Microsoft Excel to create a simple Gantt chart

- Note your start and finish date for your dissertation.
- Identify and list all tasks to be completed in column (A) in Microsoft Excel in chronological order.
- For each task listed, decide on the start date and end date for the task, giving allowance for any unexpected delays or circumstances that may affect the estimated completion time.
- Enter the start date for each task in column (B), and the end date in column C.
- Enter the time duration of each task in column D. This can be obtained by calculating the difference between the start date and end date using the formula $(=Cn-Bn)$[1] and format the cell by right clicking it and choosing 'number' in the category list.
- Start building the chart by highlighting start date cells.
- Click 'insert' from the top menu and select 'chart'.
- Select 'stacked bar chart'.

- Add the duration data in the actual bar chart, by right click-ing the chart and selecting 'data'.
- From 'select data source' menu, click 'add'.
- Your series name is 'duration' and your series data are the 'duration values'.
- Click 'edit' button to use the list of tasks to define or label the horizontal axis.
- Select the start date data by clicking any of the blue chart and choose 'no fill'.
- Re-order the tasks in your chart by right clicking on the task, and select 'format axis' from the menu, then check the 'categories in reverse order' box.
- Format the top date range in your chart.
- To do this, you need to take the earliest start date and latest end date and format these as general numbers in Excel.
- Enter these numbers in the 'minimum' and 'maximum' boxes respectively in the 'format axis' menu.

Or you might prefer to use specific project-management software. Microsoft Office Project is one such piece of software that helps you to control your work and schedule your time. Simple project-management templates can also help you. You might have come across these kinds of template as part of your personal development planning, or you may devise your own charts and milestone indicators.

Whichever approach you adopt to help you manage your time for the dissertation, you need to be honest with yourself about what you can do in the time that is available. Your supervisor will be able to give you guidance on whether your plans are realistic.

Key messages

- Dissertations can have different objectives.
- Ideas for topics can come from a variety of sources: staff, other stu-dents, past modules and essays, the media or the internet.
- Choose a topic that will sustain your interest over the coming year and one that has some background and existing literature to it.
- Your research questions should be relevant, manageable, substantial, consistent with your assessment, clear and interesting.

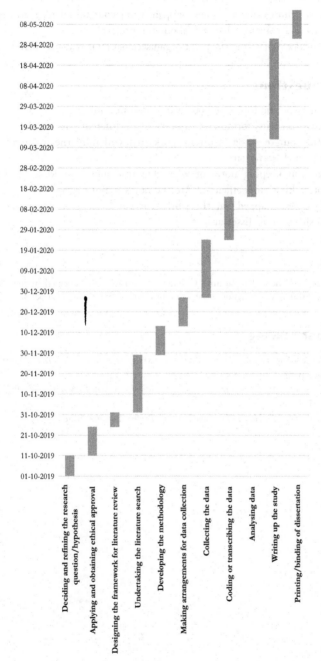

Figure 3.2 Simple Gantt chart, created with Microsoft Excel, relating to key tasks in writing dissertation

- Write things down as they happen, from your initial ideas to problems and your own feelings about the project.
- Consider project-management organisational tools that may help you.

Key questions

- What specific topic are you really interested in?
- Have you tried formulating questions in different ways?
- Will your question result in work that will fulfil the requirements of your dissertation?
- Are you keeping notes of what you read and your ideas? Is your note-taking time efficient? Are the notes useful to you?
- Have you mapped out the work that you need to do from start to finish for your dissertation?

Note

1 Cn denotes the cell in column C and row number n as indicated in the Excel sheet. Similarly, Bn denotes the value of column B and row number n.

Further reading

Allen, D. (2015). *Getting Things Done: The Art of Stress-Free Productivity*. London: Piatkus Books.
Cottrell, S. (2014). *Dissertations and Project Reports A Step by Step Guide.*. Basingstoke: Palgrave.
Thomas, G. (2017). *How to Do Your Research Project*. London: Sage.

Chapter 4

Searching and reviewing literature

Introduction

This chapter examines the essential skills in literature reviewing and offers advice on where to search for literature for your dissertation. It offers practical guide and tips on how to undertake an effective search to generate resources for your dissertation. The chapter also covers issues relating to referencing, citations, quoting, paraphrasing and acknowledging other people's work in a dissertation.

By the end of the chapter, you will have a better understanding of:

- Designing literature search strategy
- Where to search for literature
- How to access the resources you find
- What to do when you find the resources
- Who to ask for help.

What is a literature review?

A literature review is a systematic study and critical examination of completed or ongoing scholarly papers, documents and other published/unpublished materials on a particular topic to understand current knowledge. It is a useful synthesis of information and evaluation of works of other researchers to establish what is known or unknown about the subject of your dissertation. Reviewing literature offers you the opportunity to gain insights into what other people have done or said in the past that relates to your dissertation. Through this review, you will be able to understand current debates and discourses as well as theoretical and methodological issues relating to your dissertation. If you want to look at a literature review first hand, a simple way would be to look at any research journal article you have used during the course of your studies; a common feature will be a review of the literature prior to discussion of the research findings. This enables the research to be contextualised.

Why search the literature?

Conducting a systematic and thorough literature search will ensure that you find the majority of the resources that will help you to throw light on the questions you are researching. A literature search will show you whether someone has already answered the questions you are asking, or it will show you how other researchers have approached similar problems. You can develop new theories or concepts based on the evidence gathered from other scholars.

It is worth remembering that literature is more than just books; literature includes all of the following:

- Books (reference, textbooks, monographs)
- Conference proceedings
- Encyclopaedias
- Journal articles
- Magazine articles
- Newspapers
- Official publications
- Online material
- Patents
- Published video/DVD material
- Reports
- Standards
- Theses
- TV/radio broadcasts.

There is a wealth of information out there. It is really important, therefore, to have a good search strategy and evaluation method in place to make sure you find the most relevant literature for your study. Based on its format, a literature review can be a systematic review, a secondary data analysis project or an introduction to a primary research topic. Just remember that looking at Wikipedia is not sufficient to produce an essay, never mind a dissertation! You will be assessed on the quality and the range of sources used.

What makes a good literature review?

The techniques you use for conducting your literature search and the way you write your review will depend on the aim and objectives of your dissertation. While some studies may require an extensive, in-depth review of literature, others may just need a short review of existing literature. Generally, a literature review tends to:

- Show your familiarity with past research and studies on your chosen topic and related subject;
- Provide a contextual framework for explaining key theories and concepts relating to your study;
- Position your research within the general discourse and debate in the field;
- Explain new concepts or define terminologies used in your dissertation to which the readers may not be familiar;
- Describe how your dissertation contributes to knowledge, by identifying gaps that your research is designed to fill or specific areas of knowledge to which your dissertation is complementary;
- Highlight the significance of your dissertation in relation to existing studies.

A good literature review will provide a comprehensive evaluation and examination of information on the topic of investigation and present this information in a logical and orderly fashion to help readers follow the discourse, debates, arguments and research findings of other researchers. Fully referenced, it should provide a good summary of relevant scientific literature relating to other people's work by synthesising what has been done, when and by whom so that readers can have a good understanding of how research and knowledge on the topic has developed over the years. Although selective, it should also provide readers with a good understanding of the background or context to the study and how the research fits or sits within existing knowledge or contributes to the development of new ideas. It should highlight key features of theories and concepts that have been used to underpin similar studies and the key assumptions of these theories (Figure 4.1). It is also important for a literature review to be balanced in terms of its coverage of different opinions and debates. To serve its purpose, a literature review should be critical and analytical in its approach so that new ideas and understanding can be developed from the evidence (Bolderston 2008).

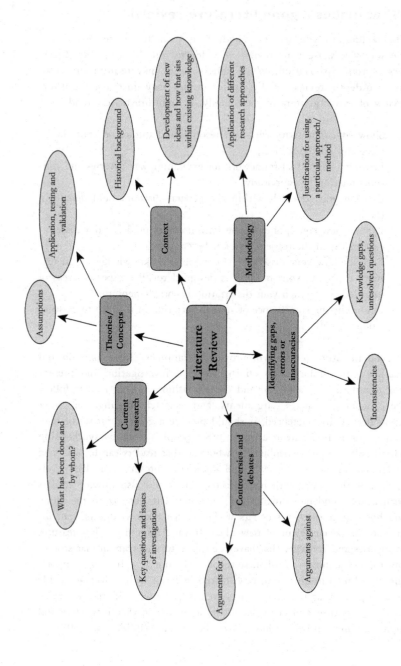

Figure 4.1 Features of a good literature review

How do I structure or organise my literature review?

Typically, a literature review should be organised in a chronological or thematical order. For a single topic study, a literature review usually requires a chronological approach where knowledge on the topic has developed over the years from past to present period (Lawrence 2011). Research that relates to different themes or multiple topics will typically require a thematic approach to literature review, although a chronological review of literature may still be carried out within each theme. Whichever approach you choose for your literature review, it is important you ensure a logical structure and flow as you weave together other scholars' work to present a coherent picture of knowledge on the topic of investigation.

Where do I find information for my literature review?

Information for your literature can be sourced in three main ways through hardcopies and online material. These are: primary, secondary and tertiary sources (Panda and Alekya 2018).

Primary sources: Some literature reviews rely on primary sources such as research reports as originally produced and published by scholars who conducted the study. These include journal articles, conference papers, theses and monographs, amongst others.

Secondary sources: These are based on literature review materials that are published or compiled by someone other than the original researcher who carried out the study. Typically, these include bibliographies, indexes and review articles compiled by a second party other than the original scholar.

Tertiary sources: Literature reviews based on tertiary sources are those that depend on search tools aimed at finding original primary or secondary literature. These include encyclopaedias, guides, handbooks and other fact-finding documents and databases.

Using search engines to find information

Search engines are programs that can search documents on the internet for keywords and then list those documents where the keywords were found. Well-known search engines include:

- Google – www.google.com/
- Yahoo – https://yahoo.com/

- Ask.com – https://uk.ask.com/
- Aol – www.aol.co.uk/
- Baidu – www.baidu.com/
- Bing – www.bing.com/
- DuckDuckGo – https://duckduckgo.com/
- Lycos – www.lycos.com/
- WolframAlpha – www.wolframalpha.com/
- Yandex – www.yandex.com

A good starting point is to search for concepts and themes on Google Scholar (www.scholar.google.com) which focus specifically on academic literature including peer-reviewed journal articles, theses, books, preliminary works, abstracts and technical reports. Many university library systems are linked to Google Scholar. If your library subscribes to the journal, you may be directed to the text via a library link after the title of the result, but if it does not, you may find you cannot access full articles without payment. It is advisable to use Google Scholar's advanced search option, which allows you to search more precisely, for example, by exact phrase, author or publication and by date. Google Scholar is only one of a number of search engines and citation databases. As with other sources, it does not offer complete coverage of scholarly works. If you are looking for citation results, look at other sources as well, such as Web of Knowledge. Other sources will use different searching options, some of which will allow greater refinement of your searches.

Essential steps in literature review

A literature review involves a series of steps and processes to ensure you gather, synthesise and critically evaluate relevant materials that reflect existing knowledge in relation to your topic. Reviewing literature is a complex process and unwieldy initial search results will often require constant review and refinement over a period of time. The essential steps in undertaking your literature review are as summarised in Figure 4.2.

Starting your literature review

The first step is to define your general topic and then to undertake a scan of the literature. The purpose of this initial scan is to map your topic area to specific themes to get a sense of what has been done before in relation to the themes or key ideas that you stated. If, for example, your topic is school exclusion and young people and crime, you will need to look at

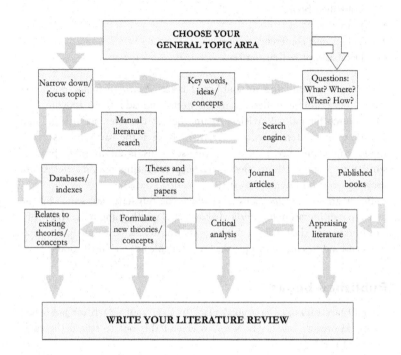

Figure 4.2 Essential steps in writing a literature review

literature on topics such as young people, education and crime and refine as and when you find useful information. You will need to think of other search terms to use; so, if you are looking at school exclusion you may wish to search for similar terms such as truancy, suspension, non-attendance and absenteeism. Although 'young people' is a commonly used term in England, remember that it may mean different things to different people (under 16, under 18, under 21?). In America the use of 'juvenile' is widely used. Your university librarian will be able to offer assistance on how to use search terms for a literature review.

Through this you will be able to identify gaps that will help you focus your topic and identify your research questions. You don't want your topic to be too broad or too vague. With your topic clearly focused, note the key words, ideas or concepts that encapsulate your study.

With your search statements in place, it is time to start your search, which could be done manually or through the use of search engines. A literature search could be based on:

- Published books
- Journal articles
- Theses and conference papers
- Databases or online sources.

You begin by searching for published books. Skim them for relevance, check their bibliographies for useful items and add them to your list. Then search for journal articles. Again, look at the reference list and add any that look interesting to your own. Repeat the same process with theses and conference papers. As you see, this is an iterative process, similar to a snowballing effect; you keep collecting relevant items and growing your bibliographical list.

Below are some suggestions as to where you can start your search for the four types of literature highlighted above. It is worth going to see your subject librarian as they will be able to point you to the best catalogues, databases and indexes for your topic that are available at your institution.

Published books

Your library catalogue is a good place to start your search for published books. However, you might want to extend this out to search the catalogues of the following:

- The Library of Congress: the largest library in the world, based in the USA.
- The European Library: this catalogue offers access to the resources of 47 national libraries in Europe.
- The British Library: the biggest library in the UK, which receives a copy of everything published in the UK.
- COPAC: the merged catalogues of major UK universities and national libraries.
- OPACS: library networked catalogues in education, research and public sectors.

Journal articles

Databases, abstracts and indexes are important sources for searching for journal articles. There are a large number of databases that you can use to search for and gather information for your literature review. Many of the databases contain collections that are subject-specific and have primary or secondary contents and articles which you may find relevant to your topic.

Using databases to find and gather information for your literature review

We have already talked about Google Scholar, other useful databases you may consult are:

Scopus

Scopus is Elsevier's abstract and citation database, launched in 2004. It is an extensive abstract and citation database of peer-reviewed literature in life sciences, social sciences, physical sciences, technology, medicine, arts and humanities. A trusted and highly regarded database by academics worldwide, it contains bibliometrics tools to track, analyse and visualise research. www.elsevier.com/

PsycINFO

Produced by the American Psychological Association, PsycINFO is a database of abstracts of literature for topics in psychology. It covers a range of materials from journal articles, books, reports, theses, and dissertations on psychological, social, behavioural, and health sciences related subjects. www.apa.org/pubs/databases/psycinfo/

ERIC

ERIC is an online digital library of education research and information, sponsored by the Institute of Education Sciences (IES) of the US Department of Education. It covers a wide range of contents and education-related articles in its database. www.ebsco.com/products/research-data bases/eric

EconLit

EconLit is an academic literature database published by the American Economic Association. It covers a wide range of contents on literature in the field of economics, dating back to 1969. It is a highly regarded database and a trusted source for economic citations and abstracts.

CINAHL database

CINAHL provides extensive coverage of literature for nursing and allied health journals. As trusted sources, nurses, allied health professionals, researchers, nurse educators and students depend on the *CINAHL Database* to research their subject areas. https://health.ebsco.com/products/the-cinahl-database

Web of science

Web of Science is an online citation indexing service originally produced by the Institute for Scientific Information and maintained by Clarivate Analytics. It provides a comprehensive citation search and links the Web of Science Core Collection to regional citation indexes, patent data, specialised subject indexes and an index of research data sets. https://clarivate.libguides.com/woscc/citationreport

The International Bibliography of the Social Sciences (IBSS)

The International Bibliography of the Social Sciences is a bibliography for social science and interdisciplinary research. It is a useful online resource and the database covers a wide range of topics in the social science disciplines, including anthropology, economics, politics, sociology, development studies, human geography and environment science and gender studies. It covers journal articles, books, reviews and chapters from edited books. https://proquest.libguides.com/IBSS

Applied Social Science Index and Abstracts (ASSIA)

Applied Social Science Index and Abstracts provides essential information for researchers in sociology, economics, politics, education, health services and allied subjects. It covers topics on housing, education, health services, nursing, social work, substance abuse, mental health and gerontology, amongst others. The database has records from over 500 different journals. https://proquest.libguides.com/assia

Sociological abstracts

Sociological Abstracts provides valuable international data on literature in sociology and related disciplines in the social and behavioural sciences. The database includes the Social Services Abstracts file that contains data on bibliographic list of current research that relate to social work, human services, and related topics. https://proquest.libguides.com/SocAbs

Theses and conference papers

Theses and dissertations are critical components of academic library research collections and literature review. Abstracts and indexes can also be used to find these kinds of literature. But there are some more specific sites you may consider for your dissertation:

ProQuest Dissertations and Theses: Produced by ProQuest, ProQuest Dissertations and Theses is an online database that provides full-text access to dissertations and theses. The database offers one of the most comprehensive collections of theses in the world with over 2.4 million records.

Index to Theses in Great Britain and Ireland: Index to Theses provides a comprehensive list of postgraduate theses and dissertations accepted by universities in the UK and Ireland since 1716 which you should be able to access through your university library.

EThOS e-theses online service: Produced by the British Library and has access to over 500,000 doctoral theses, which are immediately downloadable. https://ethos.bl.uk/

EBSCO Open Dissertations: Includes content from American Doctoral Dissertations. It is a free database with records for more than 800,000 electronic theses and dissertations from around the world. www.ebsco.com/products/research-databases/ebsco-open-dissertations

DART-Europe: A partnership of research libraries and organisations working together to provide access to European research theses. http://www.dart-europe.eu/About/info.php

Trove: Helps you find and use resources relating to Australia; it brings together content from libraries, museums, archives and other research organisations. https://trove.nla.gov.au

Using communication technologies and social networking platforms to stay abreast of new literature

Social networking platforms (such as Facebook and LinkedIn), micro-blogging sites (such as Twitter) or researchers' own personal blogs can be an excellent way to find out about the most current research in your area. Many researchers will publicise their work through sites such as these and will sometimes link you to free copies of their articles. It is worth following some of the key researchers in your area; you might even start a conversation with them. If you are wanting to keep up to date with news sources, Reddit, the social news website, will allow you to follow discussions about specific issues relating to your dissertation.

Another way to keep up to date with your reading is to set up automatic alerts that let you know that a new article has been published in your area. You might set alerts up with specific journals or through a profile on Google Scholar, for example, or a Table of Contents alerting system, such as JournalTOCs: www.journaltocs.hw.ac.uk/. Harzing (2018)'s blog gives some useful guidance on how to keep on top of your reading without overloading yourself.[1]

The bliss of browsing

The previous section has focused particularly on online searches (from catalogues to information gateways). However, you should not underestimate how productive perusing your library collection can be. It is worth spending some time browsing the shelves in the library. Once you have located a book that your search has highlighted, have a look and see what's placed around it – you never know what you might find!

Sourcing references

Having searched a number of sources, you might be overwhelmed by the volume of literature that your search produces. This is why it is so important to have defined the parameters of your topic when you begin planning your research, so that you can ascertain what is relevant to your topic and what is not. You should remember, however, that your dissertation is more than the literature that you review; so, set yourself a timeframe for searching and stop when your time is up. You must ensure that you leave sufficient time to cover the rest of your research.

With a list of references that you want to look at, you need to source those documents. If you are lucky, the document will be available at your own library. In this case, you will need only to go and collect it. Increasingly, universities have a large number of resources available in electronic or digital form. Sometimes, however, your library will not have a copy of the reference that you need. Initially, it is worth asking your supervisor if they have a copy you could borrow; if it is a key text in your area, they might well do. If not, then you need to see where the copies are held. If another library in your city has a copy, you might decide to go and access the document there. Most libraries have 'reading access' rights, meaning that you can go to their library and read the source but not take it away. You are unlikely, however, to get access to their electronic services. It is best to phone ahead and see whether it is worth making the trip.

If you are struggling to find a resource, your university will most likely operate an Inter-Library Loan (ILL) system. This means that the source you need will be ordered from another library and delivered to you. If the source is a book, you will be given a date by which you will need to return it. If it is a journal article, then you will probably be sent a photocopy by post or, increasingly, by email, but either way be aware that access will not be instant. You may also have to pay for this service, so make sure that the source is relevant for your research. At this stage, you will have access to the sources that will be the foundation to your research. It is worth checking your list with your supervisor; they will be able to tell you whether there are key references missing.

Working with sources

As you collect your list of references, you can keep a check on their relevance without initially reading them all in depth. You can pick up clues as to whether your source will be useful by reading the abstract, the conclusion and/or the contents page.

You will also need to evaluate the documents you have retrieved and the credibility of the author(s). If you are working with internet sources, you need to be even more careful when evaluating what you read because anyone can put anything on the internet (think Wikipedia!). Carefully consider the accuracy of the information you obtain from the internet and note the authorship, dates when the site was last updated and how you accessed the site.

Your institution's library may provide training on information literacy tutorial which will guide you in how to evaluate your sources. In the course of your literature review, you may disregard texts that do not meet the criteria of your study; however, you may need to refer to the bibliographies again to check whether there are sources listed there that look interesting, but which are not on your developing reference list.

It is essential that you keep a record of your sources and references as you go along, this will make your life much easier in the long run when you come to construct your reference list. Even articles you dismiss initially may subsequently prove to be of interest or useful as your ideas become more developed. There is nothing more frustrating than spending time that you do not have searching for the details of a source you can remember reading but did not record. As you collect your sources, you should be keeping a note of:

• Author
• Title (of article, journal, chapter, book)

- Editor (for edited books)
- Edition, volume, issue
- Publisher
- Place of publication
- Web page and date of access for internet sources
- Key words
- How you found the source – keep a record in your search strategies (some information databases will allow you to save searches and set up alerts).

You might also want to add in your comments on the source, to remind you at a later date why this particular piece was important.

There are different ways that you can store this information. The least technical is to make a note of details on index cards, which you then store alphabetically in an index-card box. You could, instead, keep a record in a Word or Excel document. The sorting function will enable you to quickly and easily arrange the references into alphabetical order; the find function will allow you to search for specific pieces of information.

Alternatively, you might decide to use a piece of bibliographic software, such as Endnote, RefWorks, Mendeley and Zotero or Citationsy. These tools can help you manage your references by creating a database which can be searched and organised. They will keep all of your references in one place, they sometimes link to databases and they will make constructing consistent reference lists much easier. It is likely that your institution will support one of these tools. So, go to the library, find out which one is available and sign up for some training. If you start to use the bibliographic software early in your dissertation process, you will find that it saves you time in the long run. Whichever system you use, however, you should aim to keep complete and systematic notes on your references.

Reading the references

You should now have a list of and access to references which are relevant for your study. Now you should start reading those sources critically. Look for the key themes in the documents and try and identify how the sources fit together. This process is going to be time-consuming because you will be reading a large amount of material. Furthermore, once you start your reading, you might find that some of the literature is of little relevance to your study. Don't panic; this is something that many researchers and dissertation students experience and is often a necessary part of the process. It is better to read something that is not central to your dissertation than miss something that might be an important and relevant contribution to the field.

While reading, make notes about the central themes and arguments of the book, chapter or article. Try and get a sense of the theoretical perspective of the author; this will be of use when you come to organise and present your literature review. Also, emphasise the way in which the piece of literature you are reading seeks to set itself apart from other literature. Importantly, start to think critically about the piece you are reading: what is this person trying to say and why? How is it different from the way others have dealt with this issue? This critical component is very important as it demonstrates that you are engaging with relevant literature in an appropriate manner to develop your academic discourse and that you can discriminate between different perspectives and approaches that exist within your chosen field.

Keep track of what you read and try to organise all your notes into themes. As you read, ensure that you also keep a note of page numbers. This is important if you want to come back to the source to check your interpretation and also, when you write your dissertation, you will need to include page numbers in your citations. Making a note now can stop you wasting a lot of time later trying to find an elusive quote. Good note-taking and critical reading in the initial stages of your dissertation will lead to a much more effective and focused literature review.

Moving to the literature review

The literature review incorporates the notes that you have made during the reading of the literature that you have found. It is an important part of your dissertation because it performs a number of related functions. It demonstrates to your reader that you have read widely and that you are aware of the range of debates that have taken place within the given field. It provides the proof that you have more than a good grasp of the breadth and depth of the topic of the dissertation.

The literature review can provide the rationale for the research question in the study. This can be done by highlighting specific gaps in the literature – questions that have not been answered (or even asked) and areas of research that have not been conducted within your chosen field. In this way, the literature review can provide a justification of your own research. It can allow you to build on work that has already been conducted. For example, you might adopt a similar methodological or theoretical approach in your work to work that exists within the literature yet place your actual emphasis elsewhere. In this way, you are building on work that has already been conducted by adopting similar strategies and concepts yet focusing the question on something that interests you.

It also helps to define the broad context of your study, placing your work within a well-defined academic tradition. Poor dissertations often fail to relate to broader debates within the academic community. They may have a well-defined research question, yet, without placing this question in the appropriate context, the research can lose its significance. The literature review, therefore, can add weight to your question by framing it within broader debates within the academic community.

Drawing on support from others

Library staff

Library staff are available to answer general enquiries in person, by telephone and online (by email or online form). For subject-specific enquiries, subject librarians or subject specialists will usually be the best people to help, including advice regarding special collections. To get the most out of your subject librarian, make sure you are prepared before you make contact. You may need to make an appointment to discuss your queries.

- Think about your questions and write them down in advance.
- If you have a query about a specific publication or research report, allow enough time for the material to be located – an inter-library loan may be required.
- It will help the librarian if you give detailed information about your topic and mention which information sources you have already consulted.

If you have queries about searches, think of key words and terms to start with. The librarian may have ideas on other helpful search terms.

How can a librarian help you?

The librarian can help you to identify relevant bibliographical databases to search in order to identify appropriate materials. The librarian can then help with:

- Explaining the search strategy
- Identifying keywords

- Navigating an information database
- How to save searches and results
- How to access full-text links
- How to set up alerts
- How to broaden or focus your search
- Explaining about subject terms and descriptors
- Explaining about the thesaurus for getting the best results from any bibliographical tool
- Citation searching.

Libraries have online and paper-based guidance on a wide range of information issues. Typically, these include:

- Searching databases and finding research literature
- Web searching
- How to reference (including citing electronic resources) and managing references (for example, using software)
- New developments in search tools and websites
- Academic skills such as writing effectively
- Online tutorials
- Advice and help for students with specific learning needs.

Libraries may also run training in-house on many of the above, and you may find, depending upon your individual learning style, that attending one or more of these may increase your skills and confidence more quickly than using online tutorials. The hope is that not only will you produce a dissertation that helps you to gain a good degree but that you will learn skills of information literacy that you will be able to use again and again both in your academic and professional careers.

Your supervisor

Do not forget that your supervisor is there to help you as well. They are likely to have expertise in your area and will be able to point you in the direction of some good initial sources. As you build your database of documents, check with your supervisor that you are going in the right direction. You should also share any new references that you find; supervisors will be pleased if you come across references that they have not seen before. Your supervisor will also be able to give you advice as to how you can best structure your literature review (see Chapter 2).

Key messages

- A literature review is an informative, critical and useful synthesis of research or knowledge relating to your study.
- You need to decide on the appropriate literature search strategies for your dissertation.
- Smart searching is key to success in writing your literature review.
- Be systematic in your search and keep a note of everything that you find.
- Make use of the full range of support available to you from within your institution and go and talk to your subject librarian.

Key questions

- Where can you find information for your literature review?
- Have you defined your research clearly enough in order to construct search strategies that return sources relevant to your research?
- Do you have the right skills to search for material online (journals, indexes, databases, etc.)? If not, where can you get access to such support within your own institution?
- What support does the library offer in terms of help with finding literature and other research (training courses, individual support)?
- Are you familiar with what your own library offers – online resources, books, journals, audio-visual material, etc.?
- How will you structure or organise your literature review?

Note

1 Harzing, A-W. (2018) How to keep up to date with the literature but avoid information overload, available from: http://blogs.lse.ac.uk/impactofsocials ciences/2018/05/18/how-to-keep-up-to-date-with-the-literature-but-avoid-infor mation-overload/

Further reading

Aveyard, H. (2018). *Doing A Literature Review in Health and Social Care: A Practical Guide* (4th Edition). London: Open University Press.

Booth, A., Sutton, A. and Papaioannou, D. (2016). *Systematic Approaches to a Successful Literature Review* (2nd Edition). London: Sage.

Denney, A. and Tewksbury, R. (2013). How to Write a Literature Review, *Journal of Criminal Justice Education*, 24 (2), June 2013, 218–234.

Hart, C. (2018). *Doing a Literature Review, Releasing the Research Imagination* (2nd Edition) Sage Study Skills Series. London: Sage.

Panda, J. and Alekya, P. (2018). How to Conduct an Effective Literature Review and Its Management, *International Journal of Education and Psychological Research (IJEPR)*, 7 (3), September 2018, 74–81.

WORDVICE. (2019). How to Write a Literature Review. [Online] Available at https://wordvice.com/how-to-write-a-literature-review/. Accessed 10 May 2019.

Chapter 5

Choosing an appropriate research methodology for your dissertation

Introduction

This chapter outlines options to help choose the research methodology for your dissertation. Some of the theoretical and philosophical ideas that shape concepts and models to do with research methods in the social sciences are discussed with real-life examples. The chapter shows that research is a complex and 'messy' business with lots of questions and issues to consider. Through this chapter, you will learn how to think through these complexities without feeling overwhelmed. The chapter offers essential information to help you feel confident to develop a research strategy suited to your research question(s). Designing a research strategy necessitates a systematic and rigorous approach but one that is sufficiently flexible to be responsive to the resolution of tensions inherent in the actual practice of doing the research. By the end of the chapter, you will have a better understanding of:

- Research paradigms
- Philosophical positions and their impact on research design
- Research approaches used in the social sciences
- How to justify your chosen research strategy.

Research paradigms and philosophical positions

Your research strategy has a direct relationship with the type of research question that you formulate (Van der Velde et al. 2004). Your methodological approach will also be influenced by the way you see the world, and the assumptions that you make about how to go about doing research: your paradigm.

A research paradigm is a set of common beliefs and shared agreements between scientists as to how to understand and solve a problem (Kuhn 1970). A paradigm provides a conceptual framework within which theories are developed or constructed.

Choosing the most appropriate methodological approach for your dissertation requires an understanding of research paradigms and the nature of knowledge and how we go about getting knowledge about something.

In relation to research, five main paradigms can be identified (Patel 2015).

- Positivism
- Constructivism
- Pragmatism
- Subjectivism
- Critical.

Positivists believe that there is a single reality or truth, which can be measured and known, and therefore they are more likely to use quantitative methods to measure this reality.

Interpretivists believe that there is no single reality or truth, and therefore reality needs to be constructed or interpreted. Therefore, qualitative methods of analysis are used to construct those multiple realities.

Pragmatists believe that reality is constantly renegotiated, debated and interpreted, and therefore the best method to use is the one that solves the problem.

Subjectivists sees reality from a rather subjective viewpoint suggesting that reality is nothing but what we perceive to be real, and it is a matter of opinion or perception.

The **Critical** school of thought believes that reality is socially constructed and is influenced or determined by socio-economic structures and power relations within society.

If we think just about the first two, positivism and interpretivism, the positivist believes in an objective and realist approach to research based on quantitative statistical analysis to establish causal relationships between social phenomena. This approach is based on empirical study involving formulating hypotheses that are subjected to validation or verification using objective data. Positivists usually draw on quantitative data obtained through experiments, tests, and scales. In comparison, interpretivists seek to understand how people interpret and make sense of the world. They tend to use qualitative approaches; for example:

interviews, focus groups or observations. While Figure 5.1 illustrates the essential features of positivist and interpretivist approaches to research, it should not be misconstrued as representing binary opposites.

You may feel that your research project does not fit neatly into either the interpretivist or positivist paradigm (or the other major paradigms introduced above), but it is important to engage with these philosophical positions when you justify your research questions and how you went about answering those questions using different methods of investigation.

Philosophical positions

Research paradigms are best understood in relation to the philosophical positions that define the focus of each paradigm and the key research issues they seek to address. These concepts are:

- Ontology
- Epistemology
- Methodology
- Methods
- Theoretical Perspective.

Ontology: Ontology is a philosophical belief about reality. It refers to the naming and describing of existence. It is concerned with reality and its observability and whether there is an existence that can be categorised and described. In most knowledge-gap-filling studies that rely on a positivist, quantitative approach reality is established through objectivity, hence the term objectivism is used to describe this ontological approach. However, critical realists would argue that the observation of that reality is subjective in nature. In most problem-solving research, there is no single reality. There are multiple realities that are constructed in the context of the study. Therefore, the term 'constructivism' is used to refer to this philosophical approach to understanding reality. The philosophical question posed by ontology is: *What is reality?*

Epistemology: Epistemology is a theory of knowledge acquisition. It seeks to explain how we know something. It relates to how we attach meanings to the interaction between our idea and experiences. It is a study of the nature of knowledge, justification and the rationality of belief. What we believe may not necessarily be true, hence there is a distinction between what we believe and what is proven to be true. While empiricists believe in the objective testing of hypothesis to establish reality or truth, constructivists prefer an interpretive approach,

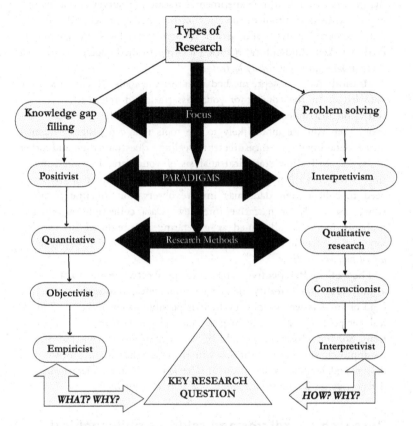

Figure 5.1 Study objectives and research paradigms – positivism vs interpretivism

suggesting that reality can be constructed and interpreted in different ways. The traditional route of scientific investigation tends to follow empirical and quantitative methods that involve data collection, hypotheses formulation and statistical analysis. The key question posed by epistemology is: *How can we know reality?*

Methodology: Methodology is a concept that relates to how we obtain the information we need to be able to construct a reality around our research. This relates to different procedures used for collecting data. In the positivist tradition, relating to knowledge-gap-filling research, the procedure tends to be experimental research or survey-based investigation, whereas in problem-solving constructivist approach, ethnographical, discourse analysis and action research procedures are commonly used. The key philosophical question relating to methodology is: *How do we go about finding out reality or truth?*

Method: As a concept, method refers to the tools we use to acquire knowledge. In the context of your dissertation it refers to your data collection instruments. If your dissertation follows the positivist tradition, then you are more likely to use tools that can generate quantitative data involving measurement, scaling, questionnaires and other tools that will allow statistical analysis of your data. If your dissertation is rooted in interpretive paradigm, then the method or tools you need to collect your data may involve observation, qualitative interview, case study or narrative interview. Data collection can involve multiple methods, all aimed at generating the required information for your dissertation. The main question here is: *What techniques do we use to find out reality?*

Theoretical Perspective: Theoretical perspective relates to the set of assumptions about reality that shapes our research questions and the kind of answers we get as a result. It is possible to use multiple theoretical perspectives in a study to pose and seek answers to different questions. So, your dissertation could be partly positivist or constructivist in its approach and both traditions will then be reflected in the way you design and conduct your research. The key question under theoretical perspective is: *Which approach do we use to know something?*

Research paradigms and taking a philosophical position

Research paradigms, as explained above, are often associated with specific methodological approaches. They are also rooted in particular philosophies about the nature of evidence and how and why particular forms of evidence may be privileged in the research process.

The social sciences encompass a broad range of disciplines. Ideas about research, therefore, are contested across these disciplines, and different views are privileged at different times by different groups of researchers in different parts of the world. So, research itself is political in nature. While you do not need to get immersed in these debates to write your dissertation, it is useful to engage with them and to understand their links with the need to justify your choice of research strategy and specific methods.

Your preferred philosophical approach

As a first-time researcher, it is helpful if you recognise your own preferences and values – your axiology – because these will influence how you collect data, how you organise it and how you analyse it. Yet, you may not realise how what you are doing is mediated through your personal frame of reference. If you recognise this possibility at the start of your research, however, you have a better chance of being a better researcher. Thinking about the way you and others may see the world differently can help you when choosing your approach. It will also help you reflect on the strengths and weaknesses of each of the research paradigms discussed in this chapter and their relevance to developing a methodology. These ideas are connected with philosophical questions that address the production, scope and nature of knowledge, which shape research and scholarly processes and activities can help you design and write a successful dissertation.

Here are some examples of epistemological perspectives that impact research.

- *Realism* is linked to ontology and the naming and describing of existence. It is concerned with reality as observable and there being an existence that can be categorised and described, although critical realists would acknowledge that the observation of that reality is subjective in nature.
- *Phenomenology* always asks the question 'What is the nature or meaning of something?' and seeks to describe things as they present to us. It encompasses a number of traditions and orientations such as realistic, hermeneutic and existential (Embree 1997).
- *Constructivism* as a form of interpretivism asserts that meaning itself is contested and that this is because 'reality' is created through the filter of our own lived experiences and knowledge so that it is not an externally driven process but is personally mediated.
- *Feminism:* drawing on understandings from constructivism, feminist researchers have developed research approaches that make explicit the humanness of the researcher and the researched. Their stance suggests that researchers must engage in critical reflexivity in order to make explicit the subjective and contested nature of meaning making in research.

Your own philosophical position will depend on your background, culture, race and experience. You will use this lens in your research, and you may find that it changes sometimes. You are likely to have shades of preference, and you should not feel that they are fixed. Importantly, perhaps, you should feel comfortable with understanding and managing *pluralism* in relation to research, at all stages from design to dissemination.

You may feel a little confused about the significance of these ideas to your project, so reading further may help as might talking to your supervisor or other tutors. Logging the fact that research is complex and contested may be sufficient to inform your thinking and actions as you progress your work.

Quantitative, qualitative, inductive or deductive approaches

You might well find that your philosophical position aligns broadly with either a qualitative or a quantitative approach, and either an inductive or deductive approach.

Brannen (2005: 13) suggests that, when designing a research strategy, 'first a logic of enquiry drives the study'. In general, deductive research is theory-testing, and inductive research is theory-generating. Often people link:

- Deductive research with quantitative experiments or surveys – focused on testing hypotheses;
- Inductive research with qualitative interviews or ethnographic work -enquiry and discovery-focused.

These links are not hard and fast; for instance, experimental research, designed to test a particular theory through developing a hypothesis and creating an experimental design, may use quantitative or qualitative data or a combination of the two. If your research starts with a theory and is driven by hypotheses that you are testing (e.g. that social class background and social deprivation or privilege are likely to affect educational attainment), it is, broadly speaking, deductive; however, much research combines deductive and inductive elements.

Bryman (2004: 542) defines qualitative and quantitative research in the following way, and he draws on the stances that have been discussed already in this chapter:

> Qualitative research usually emphasizes words rather than quantification in the collection and analysis of data. As a research strategy it is **inductivist**, **constructivist**, and **interpretivist**, but qualitative researchers do not subscribe to all three of these features.

Quantitative research usually emphasizes quantification in the collection and analysis of data. As a research strategy it is **deductivist** and **objectivist** and incorporates a natural science model of the research model (in particular one influenced by **positivism**), but quantitative researchers do not always subscribe to all three of these features.

The approach that you choose will influence the kinds of data that you collect, and the way in which you will collect it. We will talk further about quantitative and qualitative data in Chapter 6.

Linking your skills and abilities with methods of data collection and analysis

In Chapter 7 we discuss various methods of collecting data. Linked with your personal values that inform your view of the world may be the extent to which you want to use the research task to build on your existing skills or to take the opportunity to explore new skills. For example:

- Do you like talking to people?
- Do you feel confident about going to new places?
- Do you enjoy working with numbers?
- Would you have any special requirements for using certain approaches?

In the UK, universities have a legal responsibility to ensure equality of opportunity for disabled students, and, if you have specific access needs, you should discuss these with your supervisor or other supporters at an early stage so that support can be planned for and provided.

Your answers will help you think about the research approach you might wish to use, though you will also need to consider practical issues and the constraints or opportunities these may provide.

Overview of methodological approaches

In this section, we introduce some examples of specific approaches to research which are used in the social sciences. A culture of cross-disciplinarity and inter-disciplinarity in the social sciences has paved the way for promoting methodological adaptation and developments within and across disciplines. It is important to note that within each approach there will be a number of variants as researchers constantly use, critique and adapt them. We encourage you to draw on ideas and principles to inform your methodology as the scale of your dissertation means that you will not be able to apply a full-blown application of many of these approaches.

Case-study approaches

Case-study research can be well suited to an undergraduate dissertation where the main objective is to collect a wide range of information on a specific subject or a contextualised problem in order to uncover the essential social, cultural, economic or political factors underlying the subject/problem. This approach to research uses a narrow lens to build a rich or thick description of a single group, organisation or individual. A case study may utilise different kinds of data to build this picture, including interview material, observation and analysis of other materials or documents relating to the research area. The emphasis is on representing an accurate picture of the individual case and does not seek to propose generalisable results. Case studies can be used on their own or as part of a combined approach to data collection. Case-study research is often used in social work and education. In Hargreaves et al. (2018), for example, case studies of families were used to demonstrate the complexities and realities of families enduring hardship. Throughout the research project, new interventions and policy initiatives were implemented and their impact observed. While the research findings were hard to generalise to the wider population, through the use of case studies in this research we were able to assess the real-time impact of policy on hardship and the research team were able to identify catalysts of change.

Evaluation research

Evaluations usually involve discussions between researchers and programme providers to define the focus of the evaluation and the methods to be used that meet the needs of both groups. Evaluations use a range of methods and commonly adopt mixed-methods approaches, requiring both descriptive data and data that identify 'hard' outcomes, often represented numerically. As an undergraduate, if you are on a course in which work placements are involved, you may have the opportunity to contribute to evaluative activity in a small way. Given the timescales involved, you would probably need to focus upon a discrete aspect or period in the delivery of a programme, for example, within an educational, community or social welfare setting. Evaluation research, given its applied nature, is used often in social work, education, community work and social policy.

Ethnography

The American Anthropological Association (2019, online) states that 'ethnography involves the researcher's study of human behaviour in the natural settings in which people live. This process requires close engagement with the people or subject being studied in which the researcher observes, records and documents the everyday experiences of the studied culture' (Bhattacherjee 2012: 40).

Ethnographic studies use a range of methods including observation, interviews, documentary analysis and analysis of visual and other media. One main advantage of this technique of gathering information is that it is more culturally sensitive and respectful of the studied people or subjects. The drawback is that it takes a long time to be fully embedded into the culture and can be costly in terms of your time and resources. While associated with anthropological studies, ethnographic approaches are used by researchers across a range of disciplines including education, sociology and health.

Action research

Action research situates the researcher as an insider, rather than the traditional 'outsider' position and is often deployed, therefore, by practitioners, for example, in education, health or social work settings. If your dissertation is about studying a unique problem within an organisation or institution, action research could be a feasible approach to consider. You may have a part time job and seek to undertake research on a particular problem or issue that is facing the organisation that you work for. It is quite common for students on placements to undertake action research to include in their placement report.

As the term implies, action research is concerned with the action that results from the research process and the impact of conducting the research. Data collection allows the researcher to assess the impact of any action or intervention proposed. Key to this is a reflective cycle, which frames the research as an iterative, negotiated process *with* research participants from which findings emerge and inform change often both during and after the research. Examples of popular uses of action research include:

•   Participatory action research is often used in community-development work, community-health projects and development work in the developing world. Sharing planning, data collection and negotiating the nature and significance of that data as well as engaging in action from the research involves time and dedication, yet this is integral to this approach.

- Professional practice. Action research is commonly used when undertaking classroom-based research and exploring other areas of professional practice. Action research can be used to inform changes to professional practice, or to address a specific problem or question.

Visual research

Visual research is based on the idea that 'valid scientific insight in society can be acquired by observing, analysing, and theorizing its visual manifestations' Pauwels (2011: 546).

Weber (2008: 47–49) outlines some of the different ways in which images can be used in research. They can be:

- Newly produced by participants and/or researchers
- Found materials or already existing images
- Already created or belonging to participant in the research project
- Memory prompts to elicit further data (from interviews, of example)
- A means to document the research process
- A way of interpreting, representing and presenting research findings.[1]

The International Visual Sociology Association (https://visualsociology.org/online) describes the artefacts used in visual methods as still photographs, film, video and electronically transmitted images. These are commonly used for purposes, such as:

- Documentary studies of everyday life in contemporary communities;
- The interpretive analysis of art and popular visual representations of society;
- Studies of the messages, meanings and social impact of advertising and the commercial use of images;
- The analysis of archival images as sources of data on society and culture;
- The study of the purpose and meaning of image-making such as recreational and family photography and videography.

Visual and communications technologies play an increasingly important role in many people's everyday lives; therefore, the use of methods associated with visual sociology or ethnography offer relevant and interesting routes to capturing and analysing data; however, understanding the analytical tools associated with such methods may involve a lot of time, practice and study. So, what might appear to be easy and accessible data may pose challenges at a later stage in the research.

Experimental research

Although more commonly associated with the physical sciences, experimental and quasi-experimental research is also used in the social sciences, particularly in psychology. Experimental research involves controlled conditions that may be replicated and is often, though not exclusively, conducted in laboratory conditions. Developments in this field are often interdisciplinary and concerned with understanding how policy interventions designed to change human behaviour may be implemented without coercion and high costs. There are many research centres in the USA, for example, devoted to such research, and if you were interested in this type of research you would need to identify the availability of appropriate resources to enable you to conduct your experiments. This type of research usually generates quantitative data.

Policy research

The complex and ever-changing policy landscape (health, education, social care, communities) invites the need for evidence-based approaches to policy design and review. The interface between social lives, political drivers and policy formation at local to national level provides fertile ground for student researchers to undertake reviews of policy or to explore comparative questions (policy reform across time or countries), supported by the availability of material published by government departments, campaigning organisations and others.

Pragmatics: justifying your approach

Any piece of research needs to justify its approach. You need to show in the dissertation how you considered different approaches and why you chose or eliminated these. You are advised to spend some time exploring books and literature about research methodology and research methods: they will give you an overview of the different approaches available and help you to make the best choice for your project.

This chapter has covered the broad considerations in designing a research strategy. The next chapter looks in more detail at types and sources of data.

Key messages

*   Your choice of research methodology depends upon the purpose of your research and your dissertation aims and objectives.
*   Research is political in nature, and ideas and positions are contested and contestable.
*   Understanding epistemological questions that address the production, scope and nature of knowledge, which shape research and scholarly processes and activities can help you design and write a successful dissertation.
*   Think about and acknowledge your own values and preferences in relation to evidence and approaches.
*   Adopt an approach that will fit with the time, resources and interest available to you.
*   Whatever approach you settle on, you must be able to justify its appropriateness to your topic and question.

Key questions

*   In choosing your research methodology, have you considered the broader theoretical and philosophical questions that underpin your study?
*   Which research approach will best enable you to generate data appropriate to your question?
*   Have you considered all the factors that may limit the scope of your research in terms of time, resources, etc.?
*   Do you fully understand the implications of choosing a particular approach at different stages of your research?
*   Do you feel confident that you can justify your approach in a logical, coherent and reasoned way?
*   Have you sought guidance and advice from your supervisor or tutor regarding your research methodology?

Note

1 Weber, S. (2008). Visual Images in Research. In J. G. Knowles and A. L. Cole (Eds). *Handbook of the Arts in Qualitative Research*. Sage, Los Angles and London, pp. 47–49.

Further reading

Benton, T. and Craib, I. (2011). *Philosophy of Social Science: The Philosophical Foundations of Social Thought*. London: Red Globe Press.

Bryman, A. (2004). *Social Research Methods* (2nd Edition). New York: Oxford University Press.

Denscombe, M. (2014). *The Good Research Guide for Small-scale Social Research Projects* (4th Edition). Maidenhead: Open University Press.

McNiff, J. (2017) *Action Research: All You Need to Know*. London: Sage.

Scott-James, J. (2010). *Ethnography in Social Science Practice*. Abingdon: Routledge.

Pauwel, L. (2011). An Integrated Conceptual Framework for Visual Social Research. In E. Margolis and L. Pauwels (Eds). *The Sage Handbook of Visual Research Methods*. London: Sage.

Yin, R. (2018). *Case Study Research and Its Applications*. London: Sage.

Chapter 6

Types and sources of data

Introduction

This chapter discusses types and sources of data used in social science undergraduate dissertations and the kinds of data that are required to answer specific research questions. The chapter explores the nature of quantitative and qualitative data and the main sources of data used for writing dissertations. It covers both primary and secondary sources of data and all types of existing data obtainable from various sources. The chapter also provides some guidance on where to find data that you do not have to generate yourself (for collecting empirical data, see Chapter 7).

By the end of the chapter, you will have a better understanding of:

- Different types of data commonly used in social science research and their likely sources;
- How primary, secondary and existing data could be used in your dissertation;
- Possible sources of data that relate to your research topic and matching data to specific research questions.

The importance of data in dissertation writing

All undergraduate dissertations require the collection or generation of data. The word data is used here to include all types of information, text-based and non-text-based resources including numbers, photos, videos, audio recordings required to evaluate or validate a claim, test hypotheses or answer specific research questions. To a large extent, the ability to find, access and capture the right data to answer your research questions will determine the degree of success in writing your dissertation. Sourcing and obtaining quality data for your dissertation is essential to any analysis or critical evaluation. Without data there will be nothing to analyse or evaluate.

In relation to data, the key questions to ask after deciding on your dissertation topic and research questions are:

- What kinds of data do I need to collect to answer my research questions or to test my hypothesis?
- Where am I going to find these data?
- Are the data I need readily available or am I going to generate my own data?
- What method of data collection or technique is best to collect that data?
- Is there sufficient and reliable data available to me to answer all my research questions?
- Is the level of bias inherent in the data tolerable to arrive at an objective conclusion?
- Have I used a sufficient range of data to enable critical analysis?

These are some of the issues to consider when thinking of collecting data for your dissertation. The essential features of DATA in your project relate to: discovering, accessing, transcribing and analysing information (Figure 6.1). The richer your data, the better your dissertation is likely to be.

Research approaches and types of data

The types of data you need for your dissertation will depend, to a large extent, on your research design, research questions, and the type of

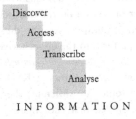

Discover

Access

Transcribe

Analyse

INFORMATION

Figure 6.1 Essential features of DATA in writing dissertations

analysis you want to do with the data. In terms of study design or approaches to analysis, a dissertation could be based on qualitative methods, quantitative methods or a combination of both. In the previous chapter we compared qualitative and quantitative approaches; here we look more closely at kinds of data associated with these approaches.

Qualitative data are based on non-quantifiable data. They tend to be text-based and cover words from your own observations, interviews you have undertaken, or from secondary sources or interviews. Qualitative research seeks to explore, examine and ultimately understand an area and is often interpretivist in nature. In this type of research, your perceptions, feelings and personal understanding of the issue is more important than any quantitative statistical analysis of numeric data. One advantage of qualitative methods is that it can be used in topics that are rather sensitive, exploratory or difficult to count. It is important to recognise any biases that you might bring in terms of your qualitative data collection.

Quantitative data tend to be data that can be counted and measured: quantifiable data. Quantitative methods draw from natural science models with strong positivist approaches. Quantitative research is based on objective facts that are not dependent on the views of the researcher; yet quantitative analysis is still subject to bias in terms of the method of data collection and the subsequent tests undertaken to complete the data analysis. With quantitative methods, the focus is objectivity based on measurable data that produces consistent outcomes or conclusions under similar situations.

Successful dissertations can draw on qualitative data, quantitative data, or a mixture of both. Your choice may depend on your preferences and abilities and the suitability of particular approaches to your chosen topic. For example, you may be interested in doing a study that is primarily quantitative, looking at social trends or policy implications. However, you also may want to introduce a 'human touch' by conducting one or several interviews asking what these trends mean to people or how particular individuals experience events. After your quantitative analysis, you may wish to include a chapter or section on the qualitative data you have collected. In your discussion of findings, you can use the qualitative data to help you understand the patterns in the quantitative analysis.

If you check out the *Internet Journal of Criminology* you will find a host of published dissertations from across UK universities. While the methods, approaches and topics are different, they do have one thing in common: they all were awarded first class marks. www.internetjournalof criminology.com/undergraduate-masters-dissertations.

Look through the dissertations and you can find examples of the types of qualitative and quantitative data that were produced to answer the students' research questions.

Figure 6.2 shows some of the main sources of quantitative data. Similarly, Figure 6.3 shows different sources of qualitative data commonly used in social science projects. Specific data collection techniques are discussed in Chapter 7 with explanations on the advantages and disadvantages of using each of the different techniques of data collection.

When you find or generate the required data for your dissertation, you need to think critically about what value that data can add to your study and the most effective way to use the data. So, understanding the nature of data is crucial to any social research.

What categories of data will you use?

When considering your research question and the time and resources available to you for your research, you have three options to consider for your dissertation. The first will involve empirical work, which means handling data you gather yourself; the other two use information and data that already exists:

1. Primary data: do I want to collect original data for my dissertation?
2. Secondary data: do I want to use data from existing research, or existing material that has been analysed as part of a research project?
3. Theoretical based: do I want to focus upon a literature-based piece of work?

Use of the third may be dependent upon the requirements stipulated for your dissertation module. Below is a more detailed overview of these three approaches.

Primary data

Primary data include information collected by you as the researcher. This is new data that has not been previously analysed or presented; it is original data. Your data could be collected through a range of different data collection tools that you have designed, including data derived from field observations, interviews or any structured survey. Generally, primary sources of data are considered more reliable than secondary data because you have control not only over the type but also the quality of data collected, and it is specific to your project. Because you collected it,

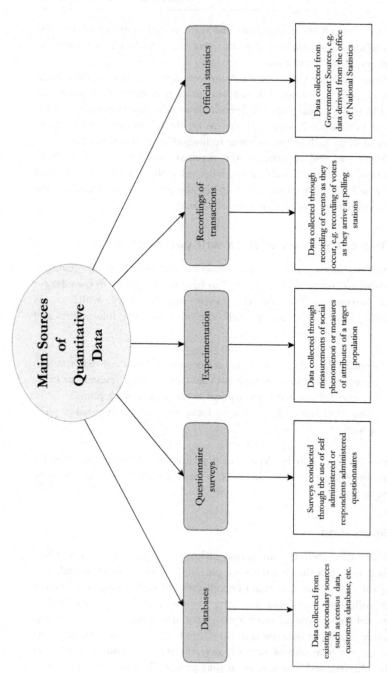

Figure 6.2 Main sources of quantitative data

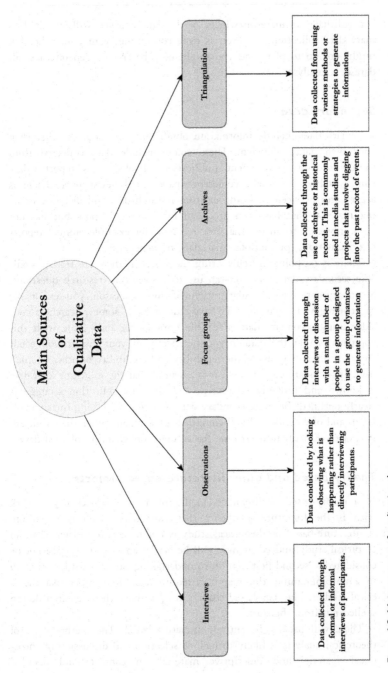

Figure 6.3 Main sources of qualitative data

Interviews
Data collected through formal or informal interviews of participants.

Observations
Data conducted by looking observing what is happening rather than directly interviewing participants.

Focus groups
Data collected through interviews or discussion with a small number of people in a group designed to use the group dynamics to generate information

Archives
Data collected through the use of archives or historical records. This is commonly used in media studies and projects that involve digging into the past record of events.

Triangulation
Data collected from using various methods or strategies to generate information

Main Sources of Qualitative Data

you will have intimate knowledge or the data, and you will own it. Primary data collection, however, is time consuming, your data collection might not go to plan, and you might only be able to generate a small dataset to analyse.

Secondary data

Secondary data include information obtainable from sources other than your own data collection. These could include data collected from sources such as government publications, books, press reports, data banks, archives, journals, conference papers and newspapers. There is a grey area between analysing existing research data and utilising existing material that has been produced for another purpose but has not been subjected to an external research lens, for example, annual reports of organisations, promotional materials, or webpages.

There is no point in 'reinventing the wheel' if there are readily available secondary data that you can use to answer your research questions. Secondary data are particularly useful if, for any reason, you are unable to generate your own data. To save cost or time, some researchers consider using secondary data a feasible option. The only issue with this approach is that the data may not perfectly fit your dissertation needs and it is difficult to assess the reliability and credibility of other people's data. If secondary data is used, it is essential that the source of such data is known and properly referenced, and the data collection strategy is clearly outlined. Because secondary data is 'second hand' information collated, and often collected and compiled, by someone other than yourself, it is often difficult to determine the accuracy or reliability of such data.

Theory-based and other literature-based projects

In a theory-based or literature-based project, the data that you work with is the literature or theory that your dissertation is based on. A literature-based or theoretical study is not necessarily 'easier' than an empirical study: indeed, it may well be harder and, again, should not be considered a 'second best' option to undertaking primary work, although in some programmes this may be a requirement. Remember that theoretical studies, like data-based studies, need to have their research design spelled out from the start.

These will usually be entirely literature-based. The methodology of theoretical analysis is likely to include selection and discussion of theoretical material and descriptive material, in context, and detailed comparison of theories in terms of their applicability. You might ask how useful certain concepts or theories are for understanding particular patterns of behaviour or for predicting outcomes.

- How useful is the concept of institutional racism?
- Is objectivity in the media possible?
- How useful is subcultural theory for understanding virtual communities?

Here, the focus of attention is not so much to discover something about the social world, for example, virtual communities, as to reach a judgement about the value of key concepts or theories in understanding that world. How the study is approached and how contrasting approaches are chosen needs to be stated very clearly.

Even if your dissertation is more empirically focused, it could still be entirely literature-based. You might choose to conduct a review of existing research related to a particular topic. What does the research literature in this field tell us about antisocial behaviour, for example? While all dissertations will include a literature review, it is possible to produce a dissertation that is entirely based on a review of the literature.

Where do I find existing research data or material?

There is a wide range of sources that provide research data (hardcopy text, online and multimedia) that you can use for your dissertation. Many of these sources will be available online.

The internet has opened up lots of possibilities for gathering secondary data and for collating existing data, for example, content analysis of discussion board messages or statistical analysis of hits on different web sites or pages and other ways as discussed above. However, depending upon what you do, there may be a range of ethical issues to consider such as those related to personal boundaries, privacy, consent and online identities (see Chapter 8) and you should keep these in the forefront of your mind.

In relation to existing research data, there are online sites and archives that provide access to data, often free of charge, that has been collected by other researchers. Here are some examples, though you should discuss with your librarian the most appropriate databases and online sources for your requirements:

- The UK's Office for National Statistics: www.ons.gov.uk/
- The UK DataService ReShare: http://reshare.ukdataservice.ac.uk/
- The Qualitative Data Repository: https://qdr.syr.edu/
- Australian Data Archive: https://ada.edu.au/
- US Bureau of Labor Statistics: www.bls.gov/

Examples of other data sources include:

- Museums, art galleries and archives;
- Websites of organisations and informal sources such as social networking sites (for example, Twitter, Facebook, LinkedIn);
- Media such as newspapers, magazines, video or other media – even non-fiction books such as autobiographies – the LexisNexis database (www.lexisnexis.com/en-us/products/nexis.page) could be a very useful source of information. With LexisNexis, you can do a full-text search of and download a wide range of newspaper materials from around the world;
- Online image sharing platforms, where you can access other people's images that may be useful, within copyright regulations and with attribution, for your dissertation (for example, Pinterest and Instagram, Flickr);
- Reports and documentation – for example, internal material generated by organisations and government reports.

If your dissertation is theoretical or literature-based, refer to Chapter 4, where we discussed literature searching. Remember that you can find relevant books and sources not only from your own institutional library, but also from national catalogues such as the Library Hub Discover for UK national, academic and specialised libraries (https://discover.library hub.jisc.ac.uk/), the French equivalent SUDOC (www.sudoc.abes.fr/), or the Karlsruhe Virtual Library, which gives access to of books, magazines and other media from library and book trade catalogues across the world (https://pro.europeana.eu/data/karlsruhe-virtual-catalog). Books and journal articles that are not available through your institution's library may also be sourced or obtained through an interlibrary loan facility.

During your dissertation, you may choose to access another library if it houses the material you need. There are often agreements between universities that allow students to access other libraries, or you may choose to work in your country's national library. The British Library in London, for example, is one of the world's biggest and richest repositories of research materials and data (www.bl.uk/visit). Access to their resources is free, but you will need to apply for a Reading Pass.

You may decide, however, that you want to collect your own data; the next chapter deals specifically with collecting your own primary data.

Key messages

- You will draw on different types of data for your dissertation.
- The type of data you collect will be linked to your philosophical position.
- Quantitative data are data (often numeric) that can be counted and measured, qualitative data (often text-based) are not quantifiable.
- Your dissertation could be based on primary data (collected by yourself), secondary data (collected by other researchers), existing data (material not produced for research purposes), or theory or literature (here data is the theory and literature you cite).
- There are a lot of secondary data and existing material available that you could use for dissertation without collecting your own.

Key questions

- Have you explored different sources of data for your dissertation?
- Have you chosen the right type of data for the method of analysis you want to use for your dissertation?
- Have you thought about and appreciated the potential value of secondary sources, rather than privileging primary data?

Further reading

Grant, A. (2019). *Doing Excellent Social Science Research with Documents*.. Abingdon: Routledge.

Largan, C. and Morris, T. (2019). *Qualitative Secondary Research: A Step-By-Step Guide*, London: Sage.

Thomas, G. (2017). *How to Do Your Research Project. A Guide for Students* (3rd Edition). London: Sage.

Walliman, N. (2015). *Social Research Methods*, Los Angeles, CA: Sage.

Chapter 7

Data collection

Introduction

When you have considered and chosen your research methodology, and thought about the types of data you will collect, as explored in the previous chapters, you will want to decide which data collection techniques to use if you are collecting primary data and plan how and when you will collect your data. This chapter introduces you to some common data collection methods used in undergraduate dissertations: surveys, observations, interviews and experiments. You will then undertake the fieldwork, which is a challenging but usually very interesting part of the research process. Planning is key to undertaking and managing data collection, so this chapter will help you to think through some of the issues and practicalities associated with responsible and rigorous data collection. Analysis of your data is covered in Chapters 9 and 10 but forms an important part of the planning stage needed before embarking on your data collection, so we advise you to read the chapters together.

By the end of this chapter, you will have a better understanding of:

* Techniques of data collection
* Data collection dos and don'ts
* Designing research instruments
* What to consider when engaging in fieldwork.

Data collection techniques for primary data collection

There are many ways of gathering your own quantitative and/or qualitative data in a systematic, rigorous and accountable way. Here, we introduce you to a range of techniques to enable you to consider preferences to explore further with your supervisor, to inform your reading of research methods literature and reviews of existing research.

Many students may think of either survey techniques or interviews as a first option, and we want to invite you to consider a broader range of techniques that may fit well within the requirements and expectations of an undergraduate programme of study. We want to encourage you to think about the rich seam of possibilities for answering a range of questions through the use of different data sources.

Not all techniques are suited for all kinds of dissertation. In selecting your data collection technique(s) you will want to ensure that the option(s) you choose will:

a. Generate the right data that will answer your question(s) both in terms of the size of the data set (neither too large nor too small) and quality;
b. Fit the resources available to you in terms of time, skills, access and costs.

Some of the most common techniques used in gathering or collecting data in social sciences are discussed below with suggestions as to when they might be appropriate to deploy. The list of techniques covers both quantitative and qualitative data. To a large extent, the type of data you need to collect depends on the research question(s) you aim to answer and similarly your method of analysis is dependent on the type of data you have collected. Beissel-Durrant (2004: 11) presents one approach for creating a typology of research methods in the social sciences and sets out categories of techniques. These are shown in Table 7.1, to which we have added suggestions for when they might be appropriate to deploy.

Here we consider the use of surveys, observations, interviews and experiments in more detail.

Surveys

Data required for your dissertation can be generated through field surveys. Field surveys constitute an important method of data collection, especially where the objective is to measure a set of dependent and independent variables in order to test for any correlation or relationship between these variables. Field surveys often involve collecting a sample of data relating to any human activity or social phenomenon using questionnaires or through a structured interview, though most rely on questionnaires. A questionnaire is a set of questions that is designed to

Table 7.1 Strengths and weaknesses of different methods of data collection

Data collection method	Strengths	Weaknesses
Observations	• Ability to record events as they occur • Evidential – if electronic recording of events or transaction is used	• Data accuracy depends on observational skills • Data/manual notes tend to be subjective and based on what is important to the observer or notes taker • Events may not be replicated to obtain similar results
Experiments (laboratory/ field-based)	• Follows logical scientific principles – inferences and reasoning • Replicable – can be repeated to obtain same results • Verifiable – peer review scrutiny • Generalisable • Generate strong internally valid data	• Weak level of generalisation • Results may not always apply to real-life situation – as real life is more complex
Case studies	• Good for testing hypotheses or interpreting theories • Can generate social, cultural, and political data to explain a particular problem • Data collected tends to be qualitative in nature and contextualised	• Reliability depends on the observational skills and integrative ability of the researcher • Difficult to establish cause-effect relationships • Not easily generalisable – as a single case study may not be readily applicable to all other cases
Action research (intervention/ consultancy)	• Allows researcher to be embedded within a social context such as an organisation • Introduction of necessary interventions or actions, based on theories, to create change • Simultaneous problem solving and insight generation • Links research with practice	• Highly subjective – researcher/consultant's bias • Not easily generalisable, as findings are restricted to the organisational context of the study

(Continued)

Table 7.1 (Cont.)

Data collection method	Strengths	Weaknesses
Secondary/ administrative sources	• Readily and publicly available third-party data • Easy way of collecting data if primary data collection is not possible or too costly	• Difficult to prove data has been collected in a systematic or scientific manner • Data not always suitable for scientific research • Weak internal validity • Difficult to establish cause-effect relationships
Ethnography	• Research rooted in the context of the subject's culture • Long time engagement with and observation of daily life of the studied culture • Allows formal and informal interaction between the researcher and participants	• Based on the narrative skills of eth researcher • Data can only be analysed qualitatively and depends on 'sense making' • Time and resource intensive • Not easily generalisable, as findings are specific to a particular culture
Surveys (field/site surveys)	• Data collected in field settings • Able to generate a large number of variables • Follows logical scientific principles – inferences and reasoning • Social problem can be studied from multiple perspectives using multiple theories • Replicable – can be repeated to obtain the same results • Verifiable – peer review scrutiny	• Difficult to establish cause-effect relationships • Nature of data is non-temporal • Surveys may be subject to respondents' biases • Accuracy of respondents claim – difficult to verify • Weak internal validity of data
Interviews (one-to-one or group)	• Flexible engagement with respondent(s) • Enables collection of rich data as interviewer can probe answers and delve deeper • Sometimes allows for discussion of sensitive issues	• High journey time and costs travelling to participants/respondents • High potential for unequal participation in group interviews • For group interview, researcher needs to be

(Continued)

Table 7.1 (Cont.)

Data collection method	Strengths	Weaknesses
	• Able to pick up and respond to non-verbal cues	confident in managing a group situation • Ample time needs to be allowed for transcription and collation of data • Not usually appropriate for sensitive topics
Interviews (via web cam/ videoconferencing)	• Closest proximity to face-to-face conversation • Bridges problems created by geographical distance • Group (or individual) interviews possible but practicalities may mean maximum four to five for a group is workable	• Problem of digital divide – unequal Internet access by potential interviewees • May experience time delays in giving and receiving sound, thus stilting discussion • Technology may not be reliable
Interviews (social media and other digital technologies)	• Online interviews possible via synchronous chat • May help to put some users at ease, for example, young people, or when discussing sensitive topics • Immediate capture of text data • Can keep digging deeper into answers	• Reliant on good enough typing speeds of researcher and interviewee • May be difficult to get in-depth answers • Lacks personal engagement
Focus groups	• Allows for the views of many to be gathered at one session • Sharing of views and experiences may enrich the data collected	• Weak internal validity of data • Not easily generalisable to other settings because of small sample
Surveys (questionnaire surveys completed by or in presence of researcher, including telephone surveys)	• Researcher has more control over completion rates • Can access answers from those who may not be able to read a questionnaire or complete answers • Statistical analyses can be applied	• Sample number likely to be smaller • Respondents may feel obliged to respond or if they receive a telephone request 'cold' may be suspicious • Types of questions that can be asked may be limited due to lack of privacy and/or direct questioning

(Continued)

Table 7.1 (Cont.)

Data collection method	Strengths	Weaknesses
Surveys (questionnaires sent via email attainment embedded or as attachment)	• Can reach larger numbers and low cost • Can reach dispersed samples • Suited to large numbers of replies • Statistical analyses can be applied	• Access of respondents to email • May need to do several follow-ups to generate enough responses • Literacy of respondents needs to be considered
Surveys (postal surveys)	• Can reach larger numbers and resources involved can be measured quite easily • Can reach dispersed samples • Statistical analyses can be applied	• Postage costs, including costs of return postage and administration time (stuffing envelopes) • May need to do several follow-ups to generate target number of returns • Literacy of respondents needs to be considered
Surveys (telephone/ radio surveys)	• Cheaper than face-to-face • Quality of data is improved if time/date to conduct interview is arranged in advance and interviewees see questions before meeting • Teleconferencing is possible with small numbers	• Non-verbal cues hard to pick up • Some people not comfortable or able to talk on the phone • Possible loss of transmission – may be hard to check out reasons for silence
Surveys (online survey platform)	• Can reach larger numbers and low cost • Can reach dispersed samples • Suited to large numbers of replies • Respondent has time to consider answers • Immediate capture of text data • No collation stage involved • Statistical analyses can be applied	• Access of respondents to email needs to be considered • Conversational style is restricted • Time-lapses may mean important response threads are lost • May need to do several follow-ups to generate enough responses • Literacy of respondents need to be considered • High costs if you cannot access free software.

Adopted from: Bhattacherjee (2012)

collect information from respondents. A standard survey will usually consist of four parts:

- A short introductory statement about the aims of the research and what the respondents are expected to do. A statement on ethics, privacy and data storage (see Chapter 8);
- Questions covering the background of the participants, for example to gain socio-economic or demographic data;
- The main questions relating to the research question, around which the survey has been designed;
- Other auxiliary or supporting questions and a statement of thanks for participating.

There are many different ways of administering surveys, as is shown in Figure 7.1. There are advantages and disadvantages of using each of these; for example:

- In a **face-to-face survey**, you can record the data *in situ* and ensure that the respondent understands what you want to do; however, this can be time-consuming;
- An **email or postal survey** can be useful if you have a large sample; however, response rates can be low;

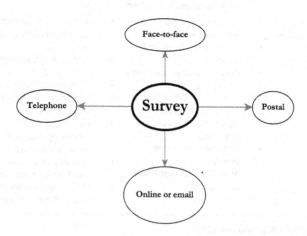

Figure 7.1 Modes of survey administration

- Telephone surveys get relatively high response rates; however, good communication skills are required;
- Online surveys are easy to set up with online survey tools and provide immediate capture of data; however, respondents need to have access to the internet.

Data collected using field surveys technique can be analysed using statistical methods (see Chapter 9). Depending on the time and sequence of collection of the dependent and independent variables, there are two main approaches to conducting field surveys:

- Cross-sectional field surveys
- Longitudinal field surveys

A cross-sectional field survey requires the independent and dependent variables to be collected at the same point in time using a single data collection instrument (e.g. a questionnaire). A longitudinal field surveys requires data collection over a longer time period. Data relating to dependent variables could be collected at a later point in time than the independent variables. The main advantage of using field surveys is that many variables can be collected during surveys thereby making it suitable for a dissertation that deals with complex issues requiring multiple perspectives. A major weakness of field surveys is that they are prone to respondents' biases as respondents may not always provide the researcher with accurate or true information regarding their feelings or views on the subject of investigation.

Observations

This approach is useful for a dissertation that focuses on the analysis of the behaviour of people or social phenomena in order to undertake some evaluation. It may include behavioural observation or analysis of people's action in particular situations or circumstances. Observational data can be collected manually using field notes or by using computer-based platforms designed to record the observations. For example, in some of our research on the police use of body-worn video (see Cayli et al. 2018), the majority of data that was collected was derived from questionnaires, yet the initial methodology was to include observing officers on duty using body-worn video while on duty and attending training events introducing body-worn videos to the officers for the first time. This would have offered an opportunity to record the conversations, comments and concerns in their 'home environment' where often subjects act more naturally and are more relaxed than when in a formal interview setting. However, similarly to when you design your own research project, we were unable to undertake this aspect of the research due to the prohibitive costs of visiting all of the police sites involved in the international study.

Interviews

Interview techniques involve formal or informal conversation which can be recorded. Interviews are a very flexible data collection technique, which can be used to collect different kinds of data. Interviews can be structured, un-structured or semi-structured. Structured

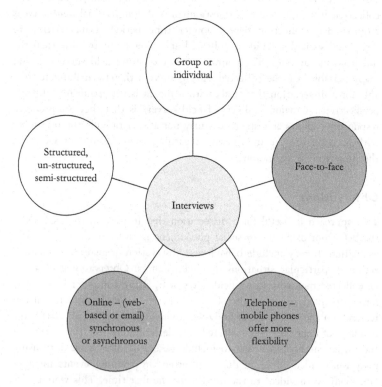

Figure 7.2 Interview modes

interviews are associated with quantitative research and will lead interviewees through a set of standardised questions (as in the discussion on surveys above). In semi-structured and unstructured interviews, you have more flexibility to deviate from your interview schedule and to explore the points that your interview is raising. Less structured interviews are associated with qualitative research. Qualitative interviews are useful for exploring people's feelings, opinions or experiences. Life history and oral history interviews focus specifically on the life experiences of people. In some visual research approaches to interviewing, interviewees might engage with or produce images to stimulate discussion (see Chapter 5) or be involved in some art-based activity, such as making collage.

Interviews can be conducted on a one-to-one or in groups basis such as focus groups. Interviews can be conducted face-to-face, online, via the telephone or email (Figure 7.2).

As with the mode of administration of surveys, there are pros and cons associated with how you choose to interview. In face-to-face interviews, for example, you can probe the interviewee and delve deeper into their responses; however, there are journey time and cost implications of meeting people in person. If you are conducting group interviews, you will save on time, but you might find it difficult to manage the group. Interviews via the telephone or teleconferencing can be more flexible as you don't need to be geographically close to the interviewee, but they rely on the technology working and it can sometimes be more difficult to develop rapport. Email or asynchronous text chat interviews provide the interviewee with an opportunity to think about their responses but can lack spontaneity. You should think through the different modes and decide what works best for your project and your potential respondents.

Focus groups are a kind of group interview. They involve bringing a small number of carefully selected people together to discuss a social issue or topic, for example a focus group to explore people's views or feelings on the legacy of former Prime Minister Tony Blair with regards to Britain's involvement in the war in Iraq. This kind of study often involves the use of a moderator (you) to facilitate the discussion so that the group stays focused on the topic of discussion. The idea is to gather information on participants' views, experiences, or comments on the topic of discussion. It is important, in a focus group, that all participants are encouraged to participate, and everyone feels able to express their views; this can be quite difficult for a facilitator to achieve. You also have to be careful that you don't unduly influence the responses from the participants.

Experiments (laboratory or field-based)

Data collected through field or laboratory experiments are ideal for explanatory research. Experiments can be conducted in various settings. While laboratory experiments are common in pure sciences, experiments in social sciences tend to be field-based and usually take place where the social phenomenon of interest is actually occurring. Laboratory experiments allow the researcher to isolate the variables of interest and control for extraneous variables, which may not be possible in real-life field experiments. If your dissertation or your hypothesis is about testing cause-effect relationships in a tightly controlled setting, then experimental studies may be a useful way to generate your data. Most experimental studies involve separating the cause from the effect in a systematic way. Data collected through experimental studies can be analysed using statistical techniques (see Chapter 9). Experimental research can be used to assess the effectiveness of interventions (e.g. across a number of schools) through a randomised control trial (RCT). This involves a similar group of individuals, for example they are all the same age being randomly assigned to two or more groups. One of the groups (the experimental group) will engage with the intervention and the other (the control group) won't. Outcomes from the groups are then measured and any difference in responses by the groups is assessed. RCTs are increasingly being used in educational research (see Churches and Dommet 2016). If you engage in experimental research in the social sciences, you should look carefully at your ethics to ensure that you aren't going to submit either your control or experimental group to harm, or that your control group isn't overly disadvantaged if they do not have access to what turns out to be a very positive intervention.

Combining approaches to data collection

Each of the modes of data collection highlighted above present their own advantages and disadvantages. You might wish to consider these and see if any of them might sway your decision to use or not use a particular technique. Some of the options may not be suitable for particular populations or because of the resources available to you. Or you may decide that it will be more effective for you to combine approaches to data collection.

If you decide to use a multi-method approach, collecting more than one set of data using different data collection methods, you will need to plan the order in which you need to collect these. For example, a focus group interview may be used to assist in formulating appropriate questions and undertaken prior to the design of a survey. In addition to the order, you also want to assess the relative importance in your study of each set of data – understanding this will help you weight the time you need to spend on each appropriately.

Don't, however, try to mix too many methods together in your relatively small-scale dissertation project; you won't have enough time or space to do the methods justice. Using five different methods will not get you more marks if they don't contribute to the overall research findings. It is much better to use fewer methods but to use them really well.

Flexibility and consistency in designing your data collection strategy

You might think the words flexibility and consistency contradict each other, so let us explain each of them a little more in relation to doing research. Designing a data collection strategy necessitates a systematic and rigorous approach but one that is sufficiently flexible to be responsive to the resolution of tensions inherent in the actual practice of doing the research. In other words, what you planned and hoped to do may not always be possible for one reason or another.

If you are undertaking research and you are trying to answer a particular set of questions, it helps to apply the same routine to eliciting answers from people. This will increase your chances of getting the types of answers you are hoping for and also lend credibility to your research. However, issues and problems often occur when conducting research, and you need to be prepared for and able to accommodate unexpected events. For example, people may cancel interviews, you may experience low response rates to a survey or weather can affect travelling plans to fieldwork sites – the possibilities are endless. Therefore, it is useful to have contingency plans in these circumstances.

If you anticipate or have problems with data collection that may impact on the data you hoped to gather or have the potential to affect completion of your study, speak to your supervisor as early as possible. This will increase your chances of finding alternatives or managing the risk and impact on your study.

Design of research instruments

Whether you plan to conduct a survey, undertake observational work, conduct interviews or run an experiment, you will be utilising one or

more 'research instrument' for collecting data. These might involve anything from a highly structured questionnaire designed to collect data
that is quantitative and measurable to the researcher or a more flexible
topic-focused interview schedule designed to elicit qualitative data of
a descriptive textual nature.

You will need to think about whether your instrument is pre-
structured, open-ended or a combination of both. This refers to questions or categories of enquiry that are coded at the design stage or at the
analysis stage.

In psychological studies, for example, you may adopt the use of
a standardised instrument for assessment or other forms of measurement.
If you are not using an 'off the shelf' instrument, then you will need to
design your own questionnaire or question schedule or observation sheet.

Even if you are designing your own, it will help you if you spend
some time looking for examples of instruments designed for other studies, including dissertations from previous years.

In particular, if you plan to use questions about respondent characteristics such as age, race or sex, you will be able to make use of the categories adopted in national surveys such as censuses. These ensure you
are conforming to current practice with terminology.

We do not have the space in this section to provide an in-depth
review of how to construct a valid research instrument for all situations.
However, we do highlight some issues that you should explore further
and explain why in many circumstances a piloting phase for the instruments is helpful, even if for you this means testing your instrument out
with friends or fellow students.

When designing your instrument:

- Keep your research question to the forefront so your instrument
  will generate relevant data for finding an answer. Decide whether
  you will need one instrument (for example, a questionnaire) or if
  you need to supplement with other methods of data collection.
- Identify your target population or intended participants. Spend time
  gathering background information about them. For example, you need
  to know where they are located, how best to access them, and via what
  mode (see below). Determine the size of your sample, and how best to
  select that sample (see section on sampling).
- Consider your mode of deployment and your audience or focus of
  enquiry (for example, if using observation) and how this may influence the design of your instrument. For instance, with self-
  administered instruments there can be little room for ambiguity,

whereas a semi-structured interview schedule will allow for a teasing out of both an interviewee's understanding of the question and your understanding of their response. Think about how people might react to your data collection instrument and whether you need to meet them in person, and how many times you might need to be in contact.

- Which sorts of questions (open or closed questions or a combination of both) are likely to elicit the best and most accurate responses? Can you use a questionnaire that has already been designed and tested by someone else?
- Have you considered carefully the structure of your questions, so you are not leading the respondent to reply in a certain way?
- Order and type of questions – surveys may require a different kind of logic than an interview schedule, with the former inviting a 'mix them up' approach of question types and item options, the latter perhaps following a more conversational logic.
- Language and presentation should be appropriate to your target population. Check readability and accessibility, for example print size and colour. If you are scanning completed questionnaires for use with analysis software, this will influence their format.
- Decide on what is a reasonable time for completion? Interviewing an eight-year-old child in a classroom setting will require the design of a short instrument, but, if you are observing children's behaviours in that classroom, for how long do you think you could maintain your attention on the task?
- Try to pilot your research instrument. When doing interviews, try to have a few practice runs first, for example, with friends or housemates. This will get you oriented into the research situation and familiar with the process. If you have designed a survey, pilot your survey with a small sub-set of your sample first. This will enable you to test out your questions to make sure the variables you have selected have been measured correctly. Piloting takes time – but it is an important part of the research process that can help make sure you don't make some avoidable mistakes. Figure 7.3 outlines the importance of carrying out a pilot survey.
- Finally, evaluate the efficacy of your research instrument. Has the instrument generated the kind of data you need to answer your research questions, and is the data sufficient for you to draw conclusions or interpretations?

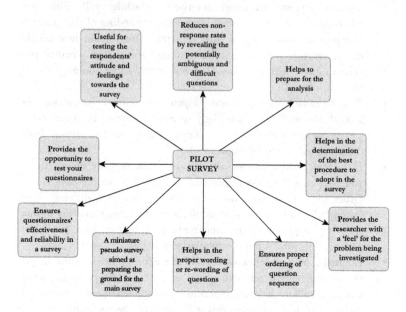

Figure 7.3 A pilot survey – purpose and characteristics

Sampling

Whatever approach you adopt, you will need to consider sampling issues. Sampling involves selection of a proportion of units, people, objects or artefacts upon which to focus your data collection from a larger set, group or population. It is important to seek guidance from your supervisor to assist you in understanding how to construct an appropriate sampling method for your research. The type of sample you choose will relate closely to your research methodology, to the population, objects or artefacts you are studying and will need to fit your resources and capacity. Big isn't always better in undergraduate dissertation sampling. A key thing to remember is to know your population and the audience you are trying to reach in your research.

A key question that often arises in applying sampling considerations relates to generalisation, that is the extent to which findings generated from a specific sample or study can be generalised to a wider population, so are concerned with external validity. You may not be in a position or wish to construct a sample that leads to this kind of validity, but your conclusions should be supported by a theory-informed and well-executed process that are deemed reliable, and for experimental and comparative studies should be associated with internal validity. This is concerned with whether the process and assessments actually measure what you intended them to.

Sample selection methods

You will need to read more widely to understand different ways to construct a sample and their different benefits and limitations in specific research contexts, but some of the common methods for selecting samples include:

- *Random sampling.* This involves selecting a sub-group from a homogeneous larger population through a process based on criteria that do not relate to any characteristics of the population (for example, choosing every fourth person or entry on a list).
- *Stratified sampling.* In a potential sample population, there may be particular characteristics or sub-groups you want to ensure are represented in your final sample. Stratification involves identifying these and then sampling from within these sub-groups. For example, you may have a class of children and you want to ensure that the 60/40% split by sex is mirrored in your sample. So, you would create a list of two sexes, then perhaps apply a random sampling approach to choosing your numbers within each of these two groups.
- *Clustering sampling.* Multi-stage sampling involves clustering what may appear to be naturally occurring groups within populations that are heterogeneous (for example, schools or electoral areas) in nature and then selecting a sample of these clusters randomly for inclusion in a study, with all units within each cluster included in the sample. So, a simple example is that schools in an electoral area are randomly sampled and pupils in the schools selected are the 'units of study'. All pupils would be sampled in each of the schools randomly selected. If these units are subject to a further random selection stage, this would constitute multi-stage clustering; for example, the sampled units are derived from a random selection of girls in each of the schools.
- *Probability sampling.* This involves setting up a random sampling approach that ensures that ascribed population characteristics have an equal likelihood of being chosen.

- *Purposive or theoretical sampling.* These involve introducing an element of researcher selection into the sample. In undergraduate small-scale research, they may be utilised for practical purposes and are commonly associated with qualitative research, where validity is not based on ideas of representativeness.

Doing your data collection

In this section we offer practical suggestions associated with doing your data collection.

Being organised

The key to successful data collection is planning and organisation. Different modes of data collection present different sorts of challenges and opportunities that impact on planning issues. For example, with surveys, a lot of the hard work is done at the design stage, formulating and testing the precision of questionnaire design, while qualitative methods involve a lot of work in collation and organising after the data is collected.

You will need to put together a timetable for preparing for data collection including:

- Organising the work associated with data collection (e.g. contacting potential interview respondents and scheduling visits or survey administration, sorting ethical approval, printing any paperwork);
- Working out timelines associated with collation, analysis and reporting of data so that you are aware of where there are possibilities to make up time if you experience any slippage with your data collection timelines;
- Maintaining an efficient and up-to-date filing and data storage system – both paper-based and on your computer for the management of data as you collect it;
- Ensuring fieldwork notes or any other material such as video or digital photographs are dated and logged as they are collected – it is very easy to quickly misplace things or forget details;
- Transcribing material as soon as possible so it is fresh in your mind;
- Ensuring, if you have scheduled a pilot stage, that you maintain your milestones for this early stage – you do not want to be running behind through the rest of the project.

Arranging fieldwork visits

Arrange the dates and times of fieldwork or site visits as early as is possible and discuss your plans with your supervisor. Give as much information in advance as you are able to, but in a style and format that is appropriate to your audience.

Correspondence, including draft email texts, should be checked whenever possible with your supervisor before sending out so that, for example, information letters and consent forms contain the correct information if your institution does not require you to use standardised documentation. Keep accurate records of your correspondence and communications; this will be important if you need to account for low response rates for requests for site visits and participation. You may need to make contact with sites in a number of ways to get a response, for example, by letter, email or telephone. Decide in advance how you will encourage potential participants to contribute to your research. Will you follow up your letters? How? When? What is a reasonable level of contact, and when should you assume silence means 'No'? There are no hard and fast rules here, so try to apply principles of fairness and reasonableness when deciding on a course of action.

When you have your visits confirmed, prepare thoroughly with your directions, transport linked with timings – so you arrive relaxed and in good time. Think about the place you are visiting and whether you might encounter any cultural differences and whether you need to modify your behaviour or dress in any way. Construct a list of all the things you need to take with you and do at the visit and afterwards, for example, sending thank-you letters.

Write down your itinerary and leave it with a colleague or friend so that they know where you should be and when. If you are concerned about confidentiality of your subjects, put their details into a sealed envelope and the details of your plans on the envelope so information need only be read in an emergency.

Many social service and health-care users have experiences of being kept waiting, and, to increase your chances of eliciting good data, you want them to be open and welcoming, not irritated by your lateness. If you are delayed, try to call in advance to let the relevant person know. Think carefully about to whom you should give your personal details, such as phone number. You may wish to keep your number hidden to the person you are calling if making contact using a personal telephone. In most situations, switch the phone off during the data collection activity.

Risk assessment

You must consider your own safety when undertaking fieldwork and ensure you have addressed any potential risks. Completion of a risk assessment form is common, and you should ask your supervisor about this if they do not raise it with you. Risk assessment is useful for thinking through the potential risks (however unlikely) that may arise when carrying out your research. You can then think through procedures for (a) minimising those risks and (b) ensuring that you have contingency plans should they arise. Potential risks include the following:

- Actual or threatened violence, psychological harm, unwanted sexual advances, etc.;
- Injury travelling to or from the research venue;
- Unfounded allegations are made against you (e.g. that you made sexual advances towards or threatened a participant);
- Being implicated in illegal activities.

The site visit

When you arrive at the site, make yourself known and, if necessary, show a form of identification such as a student letter and any communications confirming the details of the visit. During the data collection activities, depending upon the situation, think about where you are positioned. For example, for your own safety with some groups or individuals, you may consider sitting near the door with interviewees in front of you so that you are nearest to the exit. You should try to arrange interviews in public or semi-public places and avoid seeing people in their private homes. If you can only arrange interviews in the evening, take additional precautions.

If at any point during an interview you feel uncomfortable or unsafe, do not hesitate to end the interview and leave – listen to your feelings. If you are feeling sufficiently uncomfortable, this means you are unlikely to be able to elicit data effectively anyway.

You have thought about your own needs and safety in the planning process. In addition to the ethical issues covered in Chapter 8, you also need to think about the comfort and safety of your research participants, to be considerate in the way you approach your data collection.

It may help you to think about the data collection process from the participants' perspective.

- What concerns might they have?
- What do they need to know in advance of completing a questionnaire or being interviewed?

- What issues might be similar or different if you are talking with them alone to talking with someone as part of a group?
- What do you think they would like to happen afterwards?

Tools and equipment

The range of kit available to assist you with data collection is increasing as technology becomes cheaper, smaller and more sophisticated in function. This supports the use of web-based tools and mobile devices such as laptops, cameras, digital recorders and players as well as mobile phones. Obvious tips for use include:

- Ensuring your equipment is fully charged and/or has working batteries before you go
- Taking spare batteries
- Testing the quality and range of your recording/filming devices
- Having a back-up plan in case circumstances change and you have to revert to traditional methods such as pen and paper.

How can social media and information and communication technologies help during the data collection phase of your dissertation?

Online technologies may be helpful in the following phases of data collection:

Recruiting participants for your study: you could invite people to take part in your research through social networking sites such as Facebook and LinkedIn or on micro-blogging sites such as Twitter.

Hosting your online survey: there are specific survey sites, such as JISC Online Surveys, Survey Monkey, SmartSurvey, Typeform, Toluna's Quicksurvey and Voxco Survey, as well as within other software packages, such as Google Forms and Microsoft Forms. When your online survey is ready to be launched you can share via the social networking and blogging sites mentioned above.

Transcribing interviews: you could use your smartphone or an app such as RecorderHD to record your interviews, and then a web app such as oTranscribe to help with your transcription.

Managing your data: you might store your research data (or back up your dissertation work) in cloud file hosting sites such as DropBox, GoogleDrive or OneDrive (check your institutional requirements).

Looking after yourself: data collection (and indeed the whole dissertation process) can be stressful. Looking after your health is always a priority,
even when writing your dissertation. There are many health and wellbeing
apps; if you are UK based, the NHS app is highly recommended.

If you use new technologies as a means of collecting data consider the
'digital divide', which relates to an unequal access to new technologies
in society. There is still a huge gap between the developed and the
developing world, between rural and urban areas and between younger
people and older people with regards to the use adoption of new technologies. It is important to state that while new technologies can serve
as useful tools in data collection, you need to be aware of these issues as
the reliability of your result may be affected, if the use of certain technologies in your dissertation is biased against some sections of your
population of interest. Your data collection instrument should not be
unduly biased against non-users of certain technologies.

There may also be biases relating to the adoption and use of different
forms of new technologies (Elsbach and Stigliani 2018:1). Some people
consider adoption and use of new technologies as essential in an era of
modernity and information age; new technologies are perceived as superior.
This may not necessarily be the case as using older technologies may, in
fact, be more suitable for your dissertation than the new ones. 'New' does
not always equate to 'better'; neither does 'old' always mean 'ineffective'. It
all depends on your research design and what is most effective for you. An
older method of collecting data may indeed be more functional and reliable
than the new techniques. On the other hand, some technophobes, who are
uncomfortable with new technologies, often consider them as mysterious,
non-human, and complex and therefore they should be avoided. This view
again does not necessarily hold true. Some social problems can be solved
using technological solutions. The use of new technologies can significantly
enhance your research experience, and make your dissertation writing
experience more enjoyable, less laborious and most cost effective.

Key messages

- There are many different methods and techniques for collecting
  data, both quantitative and qualitative.
- All methods have strengths and limitations, so use a method that is
  a good fit for your question and situation.
- Efficient and effective planning and organisation are crucial to
  ensure you remember all the things you need to do and within the
  timescales you have set for this phase of work.

- Consult with your supervisor in the design of your research instrument(s) and sampling. Confirm that it's OK to use questions from other studies (with appropriate acknowledgement).
- Make a checklist of all the practical tasks you have to do.

Key questions

- Have you explored different data collection options?
- Have you chosen techniques appropriate to your question, skills and resources available to you, including time?
- Have you appreciated the potential value of secondary sources, rather than privileging primary data?
- Is your detailed planning in hand to ensure you can complete your fieldwork in good time to analyse and report on the data you collected?

Further reading

Bhattacherjee, A. (2012). *Social Science Research: Principles, Methods, and Practices* (2nd Edition). Tampa, FL: University of South Florida.

Cresswell, J. W. (2014). *Research Design: Qualitative, Quantitative and Mixed Methods Approaches* (4th Edition). London: Sage.

Kara, H. (2015). *Creative Research Methods in the Social Sciences: A Practical Guide.* Bristol: Policy Press.

Ritchie, J., Lewis, J., Nicholls, C. M. and Ormston, R. (2014). *Qualitative Research Practice: A Guide for Social Science Students & Researchers* (2nd Edition). London: Sage.

Walliman, N. (2015). *Social Research Methods.* Los Angeles, CA: Sage.

Chapter 8

Ethics and legal issues regarding social research and personal data

Introduction

This chapter explores essential ethical principles and the practicalities of applying these principles in carrying out good social research to help you to conduct your research in an ethical manner. Ethical and legal issues relating to the collection, storage, and use of personal data that can be used for social research are examined. We begin the chapter by explaining why matters of ethics are so central to the research process and then show you how to ensure you meet ethical requirements when carrying out research, from a principled stance to meeting formal ethical guidelines required by your institution and other related organisations. While the formal requirements and expectations may differ dependent upon the country you live in, there are understandings and rules of good social research of which all those undertaking such research must be cognisant. You will be offered guidance from your own institution around the ethics submission process. Remember that the process can take some time to complete so make sure you submit your ethics application in good time as you cannot start any research until you have received approval.

The chapter also specifically discusses the European Union's General Data Protection Regulations (GDPR) about processing personal data belonging to EU citizens. Issues of consent, anonymity, and non-disclosure of personal data in research are also explained with regards to what is legal and/or ethical. Practical guides are provided on the legal and ethical matters relating to conducting social research and how to avoid any breach of the data protection laws.

By the end of the chapter, you will have a better understanding of:

- The importance of ethics in research
- Ethical principles and morals in undergraduate research

- Ethics and practicalities in research
- GDPR and legal issues relating to collection, storage and use of personal data.

What do we mean by research ethics?

Research ethics are the principles that we use to make decisions about what is acceptable practice in any research project. Issues of morality are related to the behaviours and attitudes you might adopt in your approach to data collection and how you use your research.

Why is ethical research important?

Research participants have moral and legal rights, and it is important that as researchers we do not violate these rights. We have to be careful that our enthusiasm for getting answers to our research questions does not lead us to pay less attention to the informed involvement of the research participant or co-researcher than we should. A code of research ethics provides an agreed standard of activity for researchers, which is designed to protect participants' moral and legal rights at every stage of the research.

A code of research ethics also promotes quality in research as it is essential for the public to trust the results of research, given that findings may impact significantly on their lives. Having researchers conform to codes of research ethics helps to protect against harmful, poor or dishonest research practice, including in the representation of results. It is unfortunate that there are renowned examples of individuals failing to act in a principled way that had dire consequences for those subjects of the research, including the actions of Nazi doctors in the Second World War in concentration camps, which, in part, was a motivating factor in the development of the Helsinki Declaration, discussed in the next section.

What are the basic principles for ethical research?

The Economic and Social Research Council (ESRC) produced a Research Ethics Framework in 2016 to which all research it funded was required to comply. The framework acknowledges the diversity of the social sciences, and this means the ethical issues and complexities associated with different studies may vary considerably. Six core principles associated with social science research are set out that the ESRC expects to be addressed, whenever applicable:

- Research should aim to maximise benefit for individuals and society and minimise risk and harm;
- The rights and dignity of individuals and groups should be respected;
- Wherever possible, participation should be voluntary and appropriately informed;
- Research should be conducted with integrity and transparency;
- Lines of responsibility and accountability should be clearly defined:
- Independence of research should be maintained and where conflicts of interest cannot be avoided they should be made explicit.

Informed consent and gaining access to research settings are continuous processes. Try to demonstrate a continuous awareness of how you got around these issues throughout the research process. For example, don't just put a tiny ethics section in and forget about it: make it part of your overall research strategy.

Embedded within these principles are the commonly agreed international standards for good practice in research as laid down in the Declaration of Helsinki developed by the World Medical Association (Hutchinson 2014), with the first version adopted in 1964 and including the following areas:

- Beneficence (do positive good)
- Non-malfeasance (do no harm)
- Informed consent
- Confidentiality/anonymity.

The foundations of contemporary research ethics lie within medical research, and there are different research parameters in the social sciences to aspects of medical research. Many professional bodies such as the British Sociological Association, the American Sociological Association, the American Anthropological Association, the British Psychological Society and the British Educational Research Association have produced their own ethical codes. The emergence of internet-based research has resulted in a specialist code of ethics to support this work, produced by the Association of Internet Researchers (Markham and Buchanan 2012).

The application of research ethics has historically focused upon self-regulation. However, latterly, the emphasis has shifted towards external regulation, and, for first-time researchers, this means the choices you make about methods may need greater consideration of these contexts before you make decisions and proceed.

Research studies have to comply with all relevant legal requirements and since 2018, in the European Union, **General Data Protection Regulation (GDPR)**, requirements which regulates how companies protect EU citizens' personal data (see below).

This includes any data protection legislation and appropriate screening of researchers working with vulnerable groups of people. This may mean undergoing a Disclosure and Barring Service check, or its non-UK equivalent, and this will have a time and cost implication.

The General Data Protection Regulation (GDPR) and the Data Protection Act (DPA) (2018)

The General Data Protection Regulation (GDPR) and the Data Protection Act (2018) are the two instruments that set out guidelines on how you should manage personal data and privacy as a researcher. The legislation, under these instruments, applies to all research projects that process personal data. It sets out the rules and regulations governing the processing (holding or using) of personal data across the European Union. The regulation requires some important changes to be made to research practice and the way researchers collect and use data. Even if GDPR does not apply in your country of study, the framework is valuable for considering and applying ethical practice.

GDPR is mainly concerned with information which can be used to identify living people. If your research involves collection of data that are entirely anonymised, then GDPR does not apply. However, if you are dealing with identifiable information you have a responsibility under the GDPR to keep the data safe, keep data subjects informed and report any breaches.

The DPA 2018, which came into effect on 25 May 2018, sets out the guidelines for data protection law in the UK. It replaces and updates the Data Protection Act of 1998. It spells out how the GDPR should be applied in the United Kingdom. If the UK is no longer part of the European Union you will need to review current legislation.

The regulation provides the framework for good practice in research and demands that information and data collected and processed for research should be:

- Lawful
- Fair
- Transparent.

To ensure compliance with this regulation, the Information Commissioners Office (ICO) was set up as an independent, regulatory office. The ICO uphold the information rights in the public interest and they are responsible for enforcing the data protection legislation in the UK. As an independent authority, the ICO has the power to carry out investigations into any breach of data protection laws and can issue fines as well as advising organisations on how to comply with the GDPR. It promotes a culture of openness by public institutions and data privacy for individuals.

Personal data and notion of protection

The new legislation defines personal data as

> any information relating to an identified or identifiable natural person ('data subject'); an identifiable natural person is one who can be identified, directly or indirectly, in particular by reference to an identifier such as a name, an identification number, location data, an online identifier or to one or more factors specific to the physical, physiological, genetic, mental, economic, cultural or social identity of that natural person.
>
> (Regulation (EU) 2016/679, Chapter 1, Article 4)

Under the GDPR, there are special categories of data considered to be more sensitive and therefore require more protection. These categories could create a more significant risk to a person's fundamental rights and freedoms if the data were not properly protected or fell into the wrong hands.

These are data relating to a person's:

- Race
- Ethnic origin
- Sex life
- Sexual orientation
- Health
- Genetics
- Religion
- Trade union membership
- Politics.

Lawful basis for collecting and processing personal data

Under the GDPR and DPA, you will need a valid lawful basis to process personal data and an additional legal basis to process any 'special category' personal data (e.g. health information) and criminal conviction data. The basis for using personal data in your study will depend on the purpose of your research and your relationship with the data subject.

Article 6 of the GDPR outlines six lawful bases for collecting and processing personal data (Regulation (EU) 2016/679, Chapter 1, Article 6). These are summarised below.

- **Consent** – the data subject or individuals have given you clear consent for you to process their personal data for a specific purpose.
- **Contract** – you have a contract with the data subject or individuals that requires their personal data to be collected or processed.
- **Legal obligation** – the acquisition and processing of individuals personal data is necessary for you to comply with the law.
- **Vital interests** – the collection and processing of the data is necessary to protect someone's life.
- **Public task** – the collection and processing of personal data is essential for you to perform a task in the public interest or for your official functions, and the task or function has a clear basis in law.
- **Legitimate interests** – collection and processing of personal data is vital for your legitimate interests or the legitimate interests of a third party, unless there is a good reason to protect the individual's personal data which overrides those legitimate interests.

The legal basis you use to justify your collection of personal data will depend on the kind of personal data your research study is collecting and the purpose of the project.

What does this mean for the design of my research project?

At the outset, you have to bear in mind that your overarching responsibility is to protect the rights and dignity of all your research participants. It is important, therefore, that alongside consideration of the efficacy of different data collection methods you also understand their ethical implications and the subsequent time and workload associations. Any research that involves contact with human subjects will raise a number of ethical questions that you will need to address. At the very least you will need to ensure that the research doesn't cause anyone harm, informed consent to participate in the research must be secured, anonymity and confidentiality issues must be considered, no deceptive practices must be used and participants should be informed of their rights to withdraw or refuse to participate in the research.

Anonymised and pseudonymised data

Some of the ethical questions could be addressed through the anonymisation or pseudonymisation of data. Anonymisation of data relates to the processing of personal data by concealing the identity of the data subject through a variety of methods. Personal data sets that have been anonymised are generally considered to be out of the scope of GDPR.

Pseudonymisation of data requires the processing of personal data in such a way that the data can no longer be attributed to a specific data subject without the use of additional information. To pseudonymise a data set, the 'additional information' must be kept separately and subject to technical and organisational measures to ensure non-attribution to an identified or identifiable person.

Working with 'vulnerable' research participants

One of the first questions you need to answer is whether your research may bring you into contact with participants who may be 'vulnerable' in a legal context. In law, 'vulnerable' has a particular meaning, but this will be dependent upon the legal jurisdiction in which you are conducting your research. In the UK, this differs across England and Wales, Scotland and Northern Ireland, and internationally there is even greater variation. Broadly, vulnerable participants may include the following:

• Infants and children under a certain age (e.g. eighteen or sixteen)
• People with learning or communication difficulties
• People in hospital or under the care of social services
• People with mental illness, including those with addictions to drugs and alcohol
• People who are elderly.

If you wish to recruit vulnerable participants who meet the criteria of the jurisdiction in which you are conducting your research, then you need to consider where and how you will be interacting with them.

Unsupervised contact may require you to undergo a screening or check to ensure you do not have a criminal record that would make contact inappropriate and unlawful, and this may take time and involve a cost to you. The school or institution where you are undertaking your research is likely to insist on this if you are having private unsupervised access to vulnerable research participants.

This does not mean that you cannot do research with these populations. It may be that you can arrange supervised access to them. For example, you may interact with children in a public place, such as the corner of a classroom, or in the presence of a teaching assistant, or in some other public venue within the institution, provided you are not alone with the participant. These are issues you need to consider at the design stage so you can formulate an appropriate methodology and schedule to meet the constraints you may be facing.

Practicalities of addressing ethical issues

There are a range of issues related to research ethics and practical implications that you have to consider when designing your research project. These include:

- Informed consent
- Protection of participants
- Debriefing
- Confidentiality
- Observational research
- Deception
- Withdrawal from the research
- Data storage.

Informed consent

The notion of informed consent is very important. It refers to the need for research participants to have the right sort of information, at the right time, presented in an appropriate format to enable them to make a decision about whether to take part in a piece of research knowing the reasons and consequences. All aspects of the research that are likely to affect their willingness to become participants should be disclosed. For research involving vulnerable participants, getting informed consent may involve briefing parents, teachers or carers about the study, who may act as gatekeepers.

The term 'informed consent' is in itself contested especially when thinking about children and adults with learning difficulties or mental impairments whose abilities to understand what is being asked of them cannot be assumed or measured easily. Again, aspects of this may be addressed in law. For example, in England, Gillick competence is used to enable children under sixteen years of age to self-consent to decision-making about things affecting their lives including research consent independent of parent/guardian consent. This notion has been picked up by other countries such as Australia. Even if children can give their own consent to participating in research, however, parents and guardians also need to be informed and to give their agreement as they will often control access to a child.

It is also imperative that participants understand that consent given at the start of a study may be withdrawn at any time should they change their mind and that they should have assurance that such withdrawal will have no negative consequences for them. For example, users of social care services may feel concerned that not participating in a study may affect access to service(s), and it should be made very clear to them that this would not be so.

You may wish to design an information sheet to brief potential participants about the study. If you are asking children for consent, you might want to use pictures and colour to engage their interest. A participant information sheet should be given before asking people to sign a consent form. Your institution may have a template that they wish you to use for your study, and you should check carefully which materials are available to you and which are a requisite.

For standard questionnaire studies, where the topic of the research is not a particularly sensitive issue, it may be sufficient to include a description of your study at the start of your questionnaire, completion of the questionnaire implying consent. Again, your supervisor will be able to advise you if you are uncertain.

Observational research

Unless the participants give their consent to being observed, observational research must only take place where those observed could normally expect to be observed by strangers.

Observational studies must not violate the individual's privacy and psychological well-being. You should also be sensitive to any cultural differences in definitions of public and private space.

Protection of participants

The Declaration of Helsinki, discussed earlier, provides the guiding principles here. As a researcher, you must take care at all times to protect your participants from physical and mental harm. If potentially distressing questions might be asked, participants must have the right not to answer these questions, and this must be made clear to them at the start. If negative consequences might ensue, then the researcher has to detect and remove these effects. This might, for example, involve having telephone numbers of helplines that participants could contact if they wanted to discuss the issues further. In research with children, you must not discuss the results you obtain from individual children with teachers and parents. In all cases, you can only report back your anonymised results unless you have child protection concerns.

Deception

In most social science research, deception should not be necessary. Sometimes, however, participants may modify their behaviour if they know what the researcher is looking for, so that by giving the full explanation to participants you cannot collect reliable data. Deception should only be used when no other method can be found for collecting reliable data and when the seriousness of the question justifies it. A distinction is made between deliberately deceiving participants and withholding of some information.

Deliberate deception is rarely justifiable. Withholding of information does occur more frequently. This might mean, for example, giving your questionnaire a general title such as 'An Exploration of Social Attitudes', rather than saying which attitudes in particular you are interested in. The guiding principle is taken to be the likely reaction of participants when the deception is revealed. If participants are likely to be angry or upset in some way, then deception should not occur. If any form of deception is involved, then you need to seek ethical approval for your study.

Debriefing

When deception has occurred, debriefing is particularly emphasised, but it should be a part of all research to monitor the experience of the participants for any unanticipated negative effects. This may involve providing participants with written information describing the study, the contact details of helplines or counselling services or health-care agencies that participants can contact if they wanted to discuss the issues further, or both. Participants should also know how to contact you after the study. Generally, the inclusion of your university email address is the best option, but there may be occasions when it is not appropriate to provide a means of having ongoing contact with you. Your supervisor will be able to advise you about this.

Withdrawal from the research

Sometimes individuals may get distressed during an interview, and you must make it clear that they can withdraw from the study at any time without giving any reason. It may be that a participant decides after an interview that they have said things that they now regret. Participants should be able to withdraw their interview data in cases such as this. It is good practice in your participant information sheet to give a cut-off date up to when participant data can be withdrawn. This will normally be up to the time when you intend to start your data analysis.

Confidentiality

Here you must conform to data protection legislation, which means that information obtained from a research participant is confidential (unless you have agreed in advance that this is not to be the case). This means that you must take care to anonymise data that you obtain from participants, say in interview studies. To do this, you must not only change names but also change any details that might make the person easily identifiable. This should be done at the data-collation or transcription stage. You are required to assure your participants that this will occur.

Data storage

If you are collecting data from participants who are not anonymous, then you must take special precautions to ensure that the data is stored appropriately to ensure the participants' anonymity. This means that data files should be kept securely, and they should not be labelled with participants' real names. You will have to keep your data sets until after you have passed your degree in case you are required to produce them by your university. Interview files and other confidential material should be disposed of carefully when no longer required.

Compliance with GDPR and other legal requirements

Your approach to processing personal data collected for your dissertation should be guided by seven principles set out by the GDPR (European Union (2016): Regulation (EU) 2016/679). These are outlined under Article 5 as summarised as below.

- Lawful, fair and transparent processing of personal data.
- Purpose limitation – collection of data must be for specified, explicit and legitimate purposes.
- Data minimisation – data collection must be limited to what is necessary for your purpose.
- Accurate – personal data held or processed for your dissertation should be correct. If personal data in your possession is inaccurate, you must erase or rectify the data where necessary and without delay.
- Storage limitation – you must not keep or retain data for no longer than is necessary.
- Integrity and confidentiality – you must process data in a way which safeguards the personal data.
- Accountability – if you are the data controller, you are responsible for ensuring compliance with the GDPR principles. Note the distinction between the data controller and data processor and their respective responsibilities under GDPR (Figure 8.1).

On the basis of individual roles and responsibility for compliance with GDPR and DPA, it is important to note two categories of people relating to handling and processing personal data.

A 'controller' determines the purposes and means of processing personal data. In the context of research, the study initiator or sponsor who determines what data is collected as part of a research study is the data controller. This can be an individual, a group of people or institutions acting alone or jointly. It is the data controller's responsibility to exercise control over the processing of personal data and who carries out the data protection responsibilities.

A 'processor' is responsible for processing personal data on behalf of a controller. Generally, the processor's activities are limited to the more 'technical' aspects of data handling, such as data storage, retrieval or erasure.

You should be clear about your role and responsibilities.

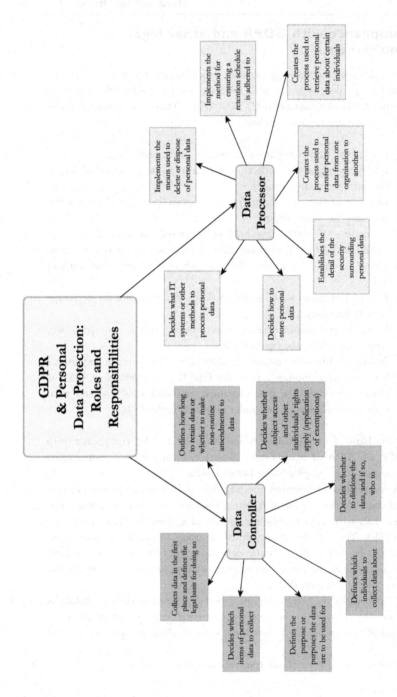

Figure 8.1 Roles and responsibilities of data controller and data processor under the GDPR and DPA (2018)

Will my research need to be approved by a research ethics committee?

To some extent, this will depend on the arrangements within your own university; however, if your research involves patients, schoolchildren or users of social care services, then it is likely that your proposal will need to undergo special ethical review even if you think there are no particular ethical issues involved. The process involved will, of course, vary considerably between institutions and countries.

Guidelines for relatively standard research proposals

While it is not possible to provide definitive guidelines, scrutiny of these questions will help you decide whether your research proposal has special ethical issues that result in it requiring ethical review by your departmental/university research ethics committee or equivalent. Your supervisor will also provide you with further advice on this. Does your proposal involve:

1. Human participants, or data from human participants? (Yes/No)
2. Vulnerable participants as defined below? (Yes/No)

    *   Infants and children under the age of eighteen?
    *   People with learning or communication difficulties?
    *   Patients in hospital or under the care of social services?
    *   People who are involved in the criminal-justice system (e.g. prisoners or those on probation orders)?
    *   People engaged in illegal activities such as drug abuse?

3. Sensitive topics (i.e. topics likely to cause significant embarrassment or discomfort to participants or topics related to illegal activity)? (Yes/No)
4. Collection of data that is not anonymous? (Yes/No)

If you have answered 'Yes' to Questions 2 and 3, you will normally be required to submit an ethics proforma for ethical approval by your departmental/university research ethics committee or equivalent.

Guidelines for the special case when patient access is required for a research study

The National Health Service (NHS) in the UK has clearly defined the criteria for NHS research involving:

- Patients and users of the NHS
- Relatives or carers of patients and users of the NHS
- Access to data, organs, or other bodily material of past and present NHS patients
- Foetal material and IVF involving NHS patients
- The recently dead in NHS premises
- The use of, or potential access to, NHS premises or facilities
- NHS staff recruited as research participants by virtue of their professional role.

All projects with NHS involvement have to be presented for ethical review to an NHS research ethics committee. Again, it is imperative to discuss this with your supervisor as you will need lots of time from the development of a firm proposal to obtaining the approval you need to proceed. Further guidance can be sourced at www.hra-decisiontools.org. uk/ethics/.

Being a responsible researcher

We have introduced you to the rules that govern ethical research and data protection, and now we want to shift the ground a bit towards the notion of being a responsible researcher. Clearly, meeting ethical requirements and conduct are part of this responsibility. However, we also want to mention other aspects of responsibility that are, it may be argued, more a question of personal morals and, to some extent, manners.

If you are involving others in your research, then you are inviting yourself into a part of their lives, asking something of people for which they will probably receive nothing in return. This raises the issue of offering some form of payment in exchange for participation. This is a contested area, and you may not be in a position to consider any kind of financial reward – for completing a questionnaire for example. However, you can show your appreciation by:

- Being on time when you attend interviews
- Where possible, giving interview respondents the chance to look at and comment on their interview material in case they wish to change anything
- Thanking people afterwards in writing or by email
- Considering ways of disseminating your research to your participants if time and resources allow.

In some circumstances, you may wish to express your thanks to people who have been particularly helpful by small gifts such as chocolates to, for example, a community worker who has helped facilitate access to youth groups. Again, if you are unsure, ask your supervisor or fellow students for their views.

Responsibility in research also involves:

- Doing justice to the data you have been able to collect
- Treating the data with integrity and not falsifying results
- Representing the views of participants in an authentic and respectful way
- Being aware of your personal biases in your treatment of data
- Engaging with others about your research and reflecting upon what you are doing, and how your actions may impact on others
- Managing ongoing relationships with research participants if you come into contact with then following the research.

Key messages

- Research participants have moral and legal rights, and it is important that you do not violate these rights.
- The General Data Protection Regulation (GDPR) and the Data Protection Act (2018) are the two instruments that set out guidelines in the United Kingdom (at 08/19) and across the European Union on how you should manage personal data and privacy as a researcher.
- There are a range of issues relating to research ethics that you must consider when designing your research project.
- As a researcher, you must comply with the legal requirements binding your actions and the privacy of the research participants.
- Consult your supervisor and institutional procedures for guidance on gaining ethical approval for any study you are considering.
- Try to continuously reflect on what you are doing and check that your actions align with those of a responsible researcher.
- Don't let time and work pressures impact on you doing the right things in terms of ethical research practice.

Key questions

- Have you sought and obtained ethical approval for your study?
- In the course of your research, have you taken the necessary steps to protect the interests and rights of your subjects?

- Are all participants in your study fully aware of the purpose of your research and how the information collected will be used?
- Have you done everything needed to protect the privacy and anonymity of your participants?
- Have you taken steps to ensure all the legal requirements and regulations relating to conducting research have been complied with and do you understand your role and responsibilities for all personal data collected and processed for your dissertation?

Further reading

Alderson, P. and Marrow, V. (2011). *The Ethics of Research with Children and Young People: A Practical Handbook*. London: Sage.

European Union. (2018). *General Data Protection Regulation*. [Online] Available at: https://gdpr-info.eu/.Accessed 22nd August 2019.

Israel, M. (2015) *Research Ethics and Integrity for Social Scientists: Beyond Regulatory Compliance* (2nd Edition). London: Sage.

Kara, H.. (2018). *Research Ethics in the Real World*. Bristol: Policy Press.

UKRI. (2018). *GDPR and Research: An Overview for Researchers*. [[Online] Available at: www.ukri.org/files/about/policy/ukri-gdpr-faqs-pdf/. Accessed 16 August 2019.

NHS. (2018). *GDPR Guidance for Researchers*. Health Resaerch Authority. National Health Services (NHS). [Online] Available at: www.hra.nhs.uk/about-us/news-updates/gdpr-guidance-researchers/, Accessed 5th May 2019.

UK Gov. (2018). *Data Protection Act 2018*. [Online] Available at www.gov.uk/data-protection. Accessed 22nd August 2019.

Chapter 9

Analysing quantitative data

Introduction

This chapter focuses on quantitative data analysis. It gives you an overview of the ways in which you can analyse the data that you have spent so much time and energy collecting. Using real-life data and examples, the chapter provides a guide to essential statistical techniques commonly used in undergraduate dissertation. By providing the essential steps and procedures in analysing your data, the chapter seeks to develop your skills in handling and making sense of your data, whether collected through questionnaires, surveys, structured interviews, observations, existing secondary data or any other methods that you may have used to collect the data. All examples and case studies in this chapter are based on real-life data. All statistical analyses are done using IBM-SPSS programme Version 24. The emphasis here is to develop your knowledge and understanding of when to use different analytical techniques and the practical skills and procedures required to analyse your data and how to interpret or draw inferences from your results.

By the end of the chapter, you will have a better understanding of how to:

- Prepare for quantitative data analysis by organising and coding your data;
- Define different types of variables and entering data into IBM-SPSS statistical programme;
- Explore the distribution of your data and using descriptive statistics to summarise your data;
- Use IBM-SPSS to construct simple graphs to visually present your data;

- Explore any statistical relationships between variables; through univariate and bivariate analyses;
- Draw inferences and conclusions from quantitative statistical analysis of your data.

Variables

Not all numbers are the same. An understanding of the differences between variables is important when thinking of analysing your data and choosing which calculations to do with your data. There are three main types of variable;

1. *Nominal.* This is when numbers are used like names. In a questionnaire, for example, certain questions might be coded with numbers to represent different categories. In a question on country of birth, Afghanistan might be coded as 1, Albania as 2, Algeria as 3, etc. The numbers 1, 2 and 3 have no numeric value and have been chosen arbitrarily. We could easily have chosen to code Albania as 9 and Algeria as 11. These categories cannot be rank ordered, and it would be meaningless to carry out certain statistical tests (such as calculating the mean) on nominal data. Other examples of nominal data include ethnicity, eye colour and housing tenure.

2. *Ordinal.* For these variables, the numbers represent categories again, but this time they can be rank ordered through the use of Likert-type scales. For example, levels of satisfaction can be numbered from 1 to 5, where 1 = extremely satisfied, 2 = satisfied, 3 = neither satisfied nor not satisfied, 4 = not satisfied, 5 = not satisfied at all. With these kinds of data it is possible to describe people's level of satisfaction, e.g. '67 per cent of respondents were very satisfied with the service.' It is important to remember, however, that the distances across the categories might not be equal. The researcher cannot judge whether someone who gives a 5 for satisfaction is five times less satisfied than someone who gives a 1. This means that, as with nominal data, certain calculations, such as mean and standard deviation, cannot be carried out on ordinal data. Other examples of ordinal data include: age categories (21–30, 31–40, etc.) or frequency of doing something (never, rarely, often, frequently).

3. *Interval/Ratio.* Here, the differences between the numbers are equal across the range. If someone is 21 and someone else is 18, the difference is three years. These three years are equal to the three-year difference between someone who is 35 and someone else who is 32. The

distinction between interval and ratio data is that the zero in interval data is arbitrary. For example, on a thermometer, the zero for Fahrenheit and Celsius scales is different. In social science research, most variables will have a fixed zero – so they are ratio variables. It is possible to carry out more complex calculations and statistical tests on interval and ratio data. Examples of ratio data include age, income, height or weight.

Think about your data and decide which types of variables you are working with before starting your data analysis. The volume of numbers from which you need to create order and meaning can be intimidating at the start of data analysis. You need to find ways to summarise the data so that you can more easily see what the data is telling you. As you describe and summarise your data, you will be making it more readable, comprehensible and clear. Here we will look at how you can describe one variable and then compare two variables. Univariate analysis is looking at one variable and describing tendencies, patterns and trends whereas bivariate analysis looks at relationships between two variables. Multivariate analysis looks at more than two relationships simultaneously.

Data exploration and descriptive statistics

Quantitative data analysis is generally divided into two categories – descriptive and inferential statistics. Descriptive statistics enable you to explore and understand your data before carrying out any further or detailed statistical analysis that may be required. For some dissertations, it could well be that all is required are descriptive statistics without any further complicated statistical analysis. There are several ways you can explore and make a judgement on the nature of your data in terms of its distribution, underlying patterns and structures. One of these may involve manual calculations of simple statistics that measure averages such as the mean value, weighted mean, the median, the mode, percentile, etc. Other manual calculations may involve the use of statistics that measure variability such as the range, standard deviation and the variance. Each of these descriptive statistics are explained below, using examples of real-life data.

Averages and measures of central tendency

You can explore the distribution of quantitative data using simple statistics that measure characteristics such as:

- Average value
- Variability
- Skewness
- Kurtosis.

Average

An average is the one value that best represents an entire group of scores or values in your dataset. Statistics based on averages tend to measure central tendency of the data. There are three forms of averages:

- The mean
- The median
- The mode.

Each of these averages will produce a different type of information about the nature of your data and its distribution.

The mean

The mean (also known as arithmetic mean) is the most common type of average computed in social science undergraduate dissertations. It is the sum of all the values in your data set, divided by the number of values or cases in that group. This is mathematically expressed as:

$$\overline{X} = \frac{\sum X}{n}$$

Where X bar is the mean value of the group of scores or simply, the mean;

$\sum$ is the summation sign denoted by the Greek letter sigma;

The X is each individual score in the group or dataset;

The n is the size of the sample or number of cases relating to your dataset. In some publications, the mean is sometimes represented or denoted by the letter M. Technically, the arithmetic mean is defined as the point at which the sum of the deviations from the mean is equal to zero.

For example, a researcher interviewed a group of ten people whose ages (in years) are recorded as 18, 18, 37, 40, 47, 54, 62, 70, 74, and 80. The mean age in this sample is 50, and the sum of the deviation of each score from the mean is zero (i.e. adding up: -32, -32, -13, -10, -3, 4, 12, 20, 24, 30).

Weighted mean

Weighted mean is used in situations where you have occurrence of more than one value. For example, a Sociology lecturer interested in calculating the weighted mean score in her Sociology and Change module over a period of three years recorded the data in Table 9.1.

The weighted mean was obtained by multiplying each score (module grade) by the frequency of its occurrence (frequency), adding the total of all the occurrences, and then divided by the total number of occurrences. The weighted mean grade, in this case, is 61.24% (6124 divided by 100).

The median

The median is defined as the midpoint in a set of values or scores. The median divides your data set into two equal halves such that one-half, or 50%, of the scores or values in your data set fall above the median point and the other half or 50% fall below the median point. Although there is no standard formula for computing the median, it can be determined by:

Table 9.1 Weighted mean of students' grades enrolled on Society and Change module 2017–2019

Module grade (%)	Frequency (no. of students with corresponding grade score)	Grade x frequency
47	5	235
50	12	600
54	11	594
60	20	1200
63	29	1827
70	11	770
71	8	568
80	2	160
84	1	84
86	1	86
Total	**100**	**6124**

The weighted mean grade is 61.24%.

- Listing all the values in order, either from highest to lowest or lowest to highest
- Finding the middle-most score
- Averaging between the two middle values, if the number of values is even.

While the mean measures the middle point of a set of values, the median is the middle point of a set of cases. In relation to the previous example and the ages of the of ten people recorded as 18, 18, 37, 40, 47, 54, 62, 70, 74, and 80, the median will be between 47 and 54, i.e. 51.5.

Percentile

A percentile is a statistical measure of distribution that shows the value below which a given percentage of observations in a set of data or group of observation fall. It is used to define the percentage of cases equal to and below a certain point in a distribution or set of scores. If a score is at the 75th percentile, it means that the score is at or above 75% of the other scores in your data set or sample. The median is the 50th percentile, i.e. the point below which 50% of your data sample fall. The 25th percentile is known as the *First Quartile (Q_1)* which is the middle number between the smallest number and the median of your data set. The 50th percentile is the *Second Quartile (Q_2)* which is also the median of the data. The 75th percentile is referred to as the *Third Quartile (Q_3)* which is the middle value between the median and the highest value of your data sample.

The mode

The mode is the value that occurs most frequently. To compute the mode, you need to:

- List all the values in your data set or distribution (list each value only once)
- Tally the number of times that each value occurs
- Note the value that occurs most often.

If every value in a distribution contains the same number of occurrences, then there is no modal value. If more than one value appears with equal frequency, the distribution is multi-modal. If two modes exist in a set of scores, then the distribution is bimodal. The mode in the interviewed group of ten people recorded as 18, 18, 37, 40, 47, 54, 62, 70, 74 and 80 would be 18.

How do I know which measure of central tendency to use?

The type of averages or central tendency measures you need for your dissertation will depend on the type of data you've collected. For categorical or nominal data such as hair colour, income bracket, voting preference, racial group, etc., the mode is a more practical measure of central tendency to use. For interval/ratio data such as income levels, age, test score, height, weight, etc., the median and mean are best used. Generally, the mean is a more precise measure than the median, and the median is a more precise measure than the mode.

Measures of variability (spread or dispersion)

Measures of variability reflect how scores differ from one another. So, for example, if a researcher was interested in the variations in life expectancy at birth across different countries around the world, they could randomly select six countries each from sub-Saharan Africa, Asia and Europe as recorded in Table 9.2.

For purpose of illustration, the life expectancy figures in Table 9.2 show different variability within each of the three groups of countries in sub-Saharan Africa, Asia and Europe. While the data shows a relatively less degree of variation in life expectancy for the selected countries in Europe, countries in sub-Saharan Africa have greater variations. The selected Asian countries have no variability in their life expectancy data at all. Technically, variability is a measure of how much each score in a group of scores differs

Table 9.2 Life expectancy at birth, total (years), for selected countries in sub-Saharan Africa, Asia and Europe (2017)

Sub-Saharan Africa		Asia		Europe	
Cameroon	59	Mongolia	69	Belgium	81
Eritrea	66	India	69	Bulgaria	75
Liberia	63	Timor-Leste	69	France	83
Mali	58	Cambodia	69	Ireland	82
Nigeria	54	Indonesia	69	Italy	83
Sierra Leone	52	Philippines	69	United Kingdom	81

Source: The World Bank, 2018. Accessible at: https://data.worldbank.org/indicator/SP. DYN.LE00.IN

from the mean. Therefore, both average and variability are used to describe the characteristics of a distribution or data set.

The three most commonly used measures of variability are:

- The range
- The standard deviation
- The variance

The range

The range gives an idea of how far apart scores are from one another.

It is computed by subtracting the lowest score in a distribution from the highest score

$$r = h - l$$

where r is the range, h is the highest score and l is the lowest score in the data set.

There are two kinds of ranges:

- exclusive range
- inclusive range.

Inclusive range is calculated using the formula:

$$r = h - l$$

Exclusive range is highest score minus the lowest score plus 1. This is computed using the formula:

$$r = h - l + 1$$

The range gives only a general estimate on how wide or different scores are from one another. They should not be used to reach any conclusions regarding how individual scores differ from each other.

The standard deviation (SD)

The standard deviation represents the average amount of variability in a set of scores. In technical terms, the SD is the average distance from the mean. The larger the standard deviation, the larger the average distance each data point is from the mean of the distribution. The SD is computed using the formula:

$$S = \sqrt{\frac{\sum(X - \overline{X})^2}{n - 1}}$$

Where s is the standard deviation, Σ is sigma – the summation sign, X is each individual score,
$\overline{X}$ is the mean of all the scores and n is the sample size of your data.

In order to manually compute the SD, for your data set, you will need to:

- Find the difference between each individual score and the mean $(X - \overline{X})$
- Square each difference and sums them all together
- Divide the sum by the size of the sample (minus 1)
- Then take the square root of the results.

The mean deviation

The mean deviation (also called the mean absolute deviation) is the sum of the absolute value of the deviations from the mean divided by the number of data points. The sum of the deviations from the mean is always equal to 0.

The variance

The variance is the standard deviation squared. This can be computed using the formula:

$$S^2 = \frac{\sum(X - \overline{X})^2}{n - 1}$$

Distribution curves and skewness

Skewness and kurtosis are statistical terms used to describe the shape of a distribution. Most statistical analysis assumes a normal distribution of data with a symmetric bell-shaped pattern as shown in Figure 9.1. With normal distribution the data tends to be around the mean with no bias

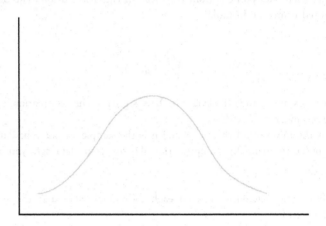

Figure 9.1 Normal distribution curve

left or right – so, for example, if you were to take a class of 50 people and measure their heights, if there was a normal distribution, then most people would have heights clustered around the mean.

However, many data may not conform to the normal distribution assumption and it may be necessary to establish the degree to which your data deviates from normal distribution. Skewness is a measure of the lack of symmetry, or the lopsidedness, of a distribution. This occurs when one 'tail' of the distribution is longer that another.

Figure 9.2 shows two forms of distribution with varying degrees of skewness. While the normal distribution curve in Figure 9.1 has equal lengths of tails and no skewness, curve A in Figure 9.2 has a longer right tail than left. This suggests a smaller number of occurrences at the high end of the distribution. This kind of distribution is referred to as *positively skewed*. Conversely, the distribution B in Figure 9.2 has a shorter right tail than left. This means a larger number of occurrences at the high end of the distribution. Therefore, curve B denotes a *negatively skewed* distribution.

The location of the mean value in relation to the median value will indicate the direction of skewness. Generally, if the mean is greater than the median, the distribution is positively skewed. Conversely, if the median is greater than the mean, the distribution is positively skewed.

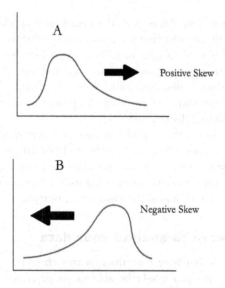

Figure 9.2 Distribution curves with positive and negative skew

In mathematical terms, skewness is computed by subtracting the value of the median from the mean. For example, if the mean value of a distribution is 95 and the median is 86, the skewness value is 9, i.e. 95–86. This means the distribution is positively skewed. Similarly, if the mean of a distribution is 67 and the median is 74, the skewness value is -7, i.e. 67–74. That will suggest that the distribution is negatively skewed.

To compare the skewness of one distribution to another, in absolute terms, the following formula is often used:

$$SK = \frac{3(\overline{X}-M)}{s}$$

Where SK is Pearson's measure of skewness (correlation); $\overline{X}$ is the mean value, M is the median and S is the standard deviation.

For example, if the mean value of a distribution is 100, the median 105, and the standard deviation is 10, its skewness will be -5. This means the distribution is negatively skewed. In the same vein, if a distribution has a mean value of 120, the median of 116 and the standard deviation of 10, its skewness will be 4. This means the distribution is positively skewed.

Kurtosis

Kurtosis relates to how flat or peaked a distribution appears. Figure 9.3 shows three different distribution curves with different kurtosis. The term *platykurtic* is used to refer to a distribution curve that is relatively flat, compared to a normal or bell-shaped distribution. A normal bell-shaped distribution is described as *mesokurtic*, while the term *leptokurtic* refers to a distribution that is relatively peaked compared to a flat-shaped or bell-shaped distribution.

Generally, data sets that are platykurtic are relatively more dispersed than those that are not. Distributions that are leptokurtic are less variable or dispersed relative to others. While skewness and kurtosis are used mostly as descriptive terms, there are mathematical indicators or measures that can be computed to indicate how skewed or kurtotic your data distribution is.

Using software to analyse your data

Do not despair if you have read through this chapter so far and wondered how on earth you would be able to do all of the mathematical calculations and produce the complicated curves, tables and graphs you need for your dissertation – there is software to help you!

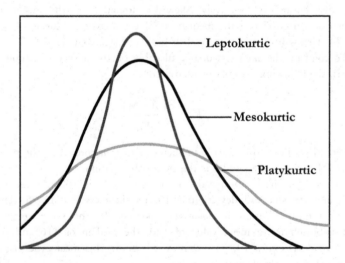

Figure 9.3 Distribution curves and kurtosis

The most commonly used statistical computer program designed originally for social scientists is IBM-SPSS. It is relatively easy to use and there are many good books that will introduce you to the program and provide step-by-step guides on how you can use it to analyse your data. While it is out of the scope of this book to provide you with the training and skills to use IBM-SPSS, we have, where necessary, offered some tips to get you started. IBM-SPSS is a powerful piece of software which has functionality way beyond what you will need for your research. Your institution might well have a licence for IBM-SPSS or other similar general-purpose statistical software such as Stata. There are many online guides, textbooks and chapters in data analysis books that may also help you with learning IBM-SPSS. It is worth taking a look at these texts and working through some of the examples before you start to analyse your own data.

There are other statistical packages available to you, some of which are free access – for example, Openstat and Excel in the Microsoft Office package. The statistics functionality of these programs is good, and the freely available add-ons can give more advanced features. Using IBM-SPSS or any of the other statistical programs will enable you to do different calculations and you can also produce graphs, plots and tables to visually present your data. For the rest of this chapter, we have provided a number of case studies to illustrate how to use IBM-SPSS to analyse your data.

The computer package only works with what you input. So, it is important you understand the principles and techniques for using IBM-SPSS to achieve your data analysis objective or indeed any other statistical package. That is why we have concentrated more on what the different techniques show rather than demonstrating how you carry them out in different packages. It is really important, therefore, that you understand the tests you are asking IBM-SPSS software to do and how to interpret the results and present your own findings. Read, carefully, each of the following case studies and examples of how IBM-SPSS was used to answer specific research questions.

Preparing data for computer analysis

The first stage in using computers to analyse your data is getting the data into a format that a computer can read. This usually involves creating a spreadsheet to input all your data. This initial data organisation could be done using Microsoft Excel or any specialised software that allows data entry and storage. If your data collection instrument is a questionnaire, you may need to design a coding scheme to enter all your questionnaire data in a format that the computer will be able to read and process the information. This initial questionnaire data management and organisation is referred to as coding.

Coding and coding schemes

Coding is the transformation of the information contained in your questionnaires into a numeric or alpha-numeric format that a computer can understand and use in statistical analysis. It relates to the method of assigning numerical values/symbols to various answer categories in a questionnaire. For each response option to a question, a letter code (a, b, c) or preferably numerical code (1, 2, 3) is usually assigned. Coding is an important stage in data processing; hence care should be taken while assigning codes to your questionnaire information to make your analysis meaningful.

For example, in a questionnaire survey of undergraduate students' educational experience and course choice in a UK University, the coding scheme in Table 9.3 was used to record and enter some of the respondents' answers to the survey questions.

The essence of a coding scheme is to facilitate computer data entry and to ensure data is correctly entered. The coding scheme allows questionnaire information to be entered in a consistent format that can be read and analysed by computer programmes such as IBM-SPSS in the form of a spreadsheet.

Introducing IBM-SPSS, defining variables and inputting data

To make the most of IBM-SPSS, you need to first know how the program works and the various interface to use it to analyse your data. It is worth consulting books that introduce you to the program in full and that helps you learn how to use IBM-SPSS software to define your variables, input your data and save your data file. To get you started, here are some useful tips:

- Log on to IBM-SPSS.
- A dialogue box will appear to either open an existing SPSS data file or create a new data file.
- To create a new SPSS data file, you need to define each of your variables in the variable window.

Table 9.3 Sample coding scheme used in a survey of students' educational experience and course choice in a UK university

Survey question	Variable name used to define question	Possible response options to question	Codes used to define options
Gender	Gender	Male	1
		Female	2
Your age category	Age	18-21	1
		21-25	2
		25-35	3
		35-45	4
		45-55	5
		55-60	6
		60-65	7
		65 plus	8
Studentship status	Status	Undergraduate	1
		Postgraduate	2
		Other	3
Mode of study	Study mode	Full time	1
		Part time	2
		Distance learning	3
		E-learning	4
		Other	5
Current stage/year of study	Study stage	Year 1	1
		Year 2	2
		Year 3	3
		Year 4	4
		Other Year	5
How important is the course design a factor in choosing your programme?	Course design	Very important	1
		Important	2
		Not important	3
How important is the University reputation and standing in the League table in choosing your course?	Uni reputation	Very important	1
		Important	2
		Not important	3

(Continued)

Table 9.3 (Cont.)

Survey question	Variable name used to define question	Possible response options to question	Codes used to define options
How important to you is job prospect in choosing your course?	Job prospect	Very important	1
		Important	2
		Not important	3

Source: extract from a student experience survey (Jegede, 2018)

- At the bottom left hand corner, you can swap between variable view window and data view window.
- In the first row of the variable view window, define your first variable by specifying the variable name (variable name cannot be more than eight characters).
- Choose the variable type (numeric for numbers or strings for texts or letters).
- Define the width of your variable – variable width must be equal to or greater than the largest number of digits in the data set for the variable including the decimal point. For example, to enter 267.84 will require a variable width of 6 while 7.9 is 3 in width.
- Define the number of decimal places in your data set. The programme default is two decimal places, but this can be changed as required. If there is no decimal place, the value of zero should be entered.
- Label your variable if required. (You have the option to label your variable with a longer name containing more information.)
- To define other variables, repeat the above procedure on row two, row three, etc.
- Once you have defined and entered all the essential information for each of your variables, you can click on the data view tab in the bottom left hand corner, to start entering your data.
- Remember to save your data.
- If a variable name is not fully displayed, you can increase the width of the field by holding down the left button on the variable name cell and dragging it to the right.

- The main menu options are located at the top of the screen where you will select all the SPSS commands needed for your analysis.

All the tips provided in this book are based on IBM-SPSS Statistics Version 24. For a practical guide to computing descriptive statistics using real-life data, read case study 9.1. It illustrates how IBM-SPSS can be used to generate descriptive statistics to summarise your data.

Case Study 9.1   Computing descriptive statistics using crime data derived from the Crime Survey for England and Wales and Police Recorded Crime Data

Problem definition

A criminologist interested in analysing the volume of violent crime dealt with by the police from year ending March 2003 to year ending March 2015 in England and Wales extracted the data in Table 9.2 from the Crime Survey data for England and Wales. The objective is to use IBM-SPSS descriptive statistics to analyse and summarise the data.

See Table 9.4
Tips for IBM-SPSS procedure for computing descriptive statistics:

- Log on and enter your data into IBM-SPSS.
- Define your variables, e.g. crime figures (numeric); crime record period (string); crime category (string), e.g. violence with injury = 1; violence without injury = 2; stalking and harassment = 3.
- Data – split file, compare groups, groups based on crime category.
- Analyse.
- Descriptive statistics; crime figures.
- Options – check mean, sum, std deviation, minimum, maximum, range, kurtosis and skewness boxes.
- Extract results from IBM-SPSS output window.

The result of the SPSS descriptive statistics computed using this data is summarised in Table 9.3. The researcher also used the same data to construct a histogram and boxplots for each of the crime category as shown in Figure 9.4 and Figure 9.5.

Tips for IBM-SPSS procedure for boxplots:

- Log on and enter your data into IBM-SPSS.
- Define your variables, e.g. crime figures (numeric); crime record period (string); crime category (string), e.g. violence with injury = 1; violence without injury = 2; stalking and harassment = 3.
- Graph > legacy dialogues > boxplot > simple.
- Select summaries for groups of cases.
- Define.
- A new dialogue box opens up.
- Move crime figures variable into variable box.
- Move crime category variable into category axis.
- Move crime record period variable into label cases by box.
- Click OK.
- Copy your boxplots and note the size of each of the boxplots, the location of the median line, the length of the whiskers and any outliers.

Table 9.4 Volume of violent crime dealt with by the police from year ending March 2003 to year ending March 2015

Period	Violence with injury	Violence without injury	Stalking and harassment	Total violence
April02-March03	371,774	302,450	33,002	708,742
April03-March04	457,223	300,090	40,522	799,247
April04-March05	514,638	277,569	52,117	845,673
April05-March06	543,044	237,218	57,192	838,674
April06-March07	505,848	249,632	58,150	814,865
April07-March08	451,806	241,226	54,531	748,779
April08-March09	420,184	236,943	50,758	709,008
April09-March10	400,703	241,818	55,329	699,011

(Continued)

Table 9.4 (Cont.)

Period	Violence with injury	Violence without injury	Stalking and harassment	Total violence
April 10-March 11	367,847	243,426	53,144	665,486
April 11-March 12	337,709	238,276	49,766	626,720
April 012-March 13	311,740	232,466	56,032	601,141
April 13-March 14	322,362	248,616	62,656	634,625
April 14-March 15	373,509	317,166	86,368	778,172

Data extracted from the Crime Survey for England and Wales and Police Recorded Crime Data.
Office of National Statistics. Accessed 4 June 2019 from: www.ons.gov.uk/peoplepopula tionandcommunity/crimeandjustice/datasets/crimeinenglandandwalesbulletintables.
(Data used for this exercise is based on Police recorded crime, Home Office, licensed under the Open Government Licence and available from Office of National Statistics. Accessed 4 June 2019 from: www.ons.gov.uk/peoplepopulationandcommunity/crimeand justice/datasets/crimeinenglandandwalesbulletintables)

The result of the SPSS descriptive statistics used in Case study 9.1 is summarised in Table 9.5. Using the same data, construct a histogram for each of the crime categories as shown in Figure 9.4.

Graphs and graphical display of data

Visual aids are an important part of data exploration and can help you make sense of your data. Graphs generated through IBM-SPSS or Excel can help you summarise your data and highlight key areas that you may focus your attention. Different types of graphs can be used to make your data more visually appealing and accessible.

The most common types of graphs used in dissertations are:

- Histogram
- Bar graph
- Line graph
- Pie chart
- Box plots.

Table 9.5 Summary of descriptive statistics for violent crime, England and
Wales, from year ending March 2003 to year ending March 2015

	Violence with injury	Violence without injury	Stalking and harassment	Total
Sample size n	13	13	13	13
Minimum	311,740	23,2466	33,002	33,002
Maximum	543,044	317,166	86,368	543,044
Mean (arithmetic)	413,722.08	258,992.00	54,582.08	242,432.05
Standard deviation	75,804.35	29,507.28	12,271.53	156,014.40
Sum	5,378,387	3,366,896	709,567	9,454,850
Range	231,304	84,700	53,366	510,042
Skewness	0.36	1.11	1.05	117
Kurtosis	-1.08	-0.40	3.87	-1.081

Source: Extracts from IBM-SPSS Descriptive Statistics Output.

Frequency distributions

One way of presenting your data is through frequency distributions.
This will show the number of people and the percentage for each category in your variable. Frequency distributions can be used for all types
of variable (nominal, ordinal, interval/ratio) mentioned above. The way
you present your frequency distribution will depend on the variables you
are describing. You can present your data in tables or graphs (pie charts,
bar charts, histograms). A good rule of thumb is to use a table unless
a graph can put across the message more clearly.

Boxplot

The box plot shows all of the following:

- The smallest observation (the bottom horizontal line)
- The bottom 25% (the section between the lowest observation and
  the grey box)
- The interquartile range (the grey box)
- The mean (thick black line inside the box)
- The top 25% (section above the grey box)
- The highest observation (upper horizontal line).

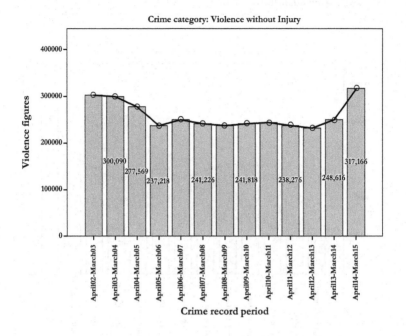

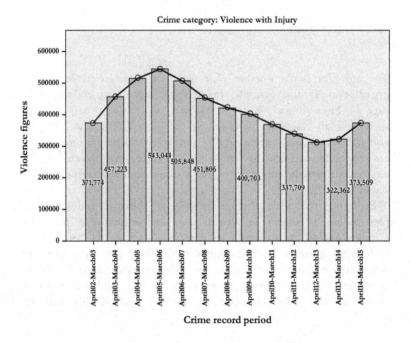

Figure 9.4 Histogram of violent crime in England and Wales 2003–2015

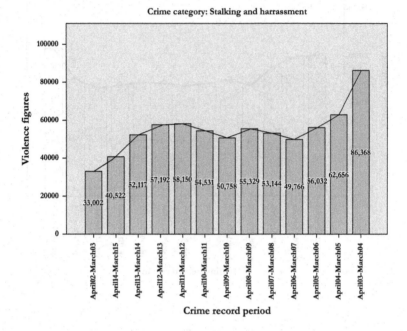

Figure 9.4 (Continued)

The box plot shows whether your data is a symmetrical or skewed distribution. In this example, the boxplot shows that violent crime data in England and Wales is skewed, suggesting there is more spread for all categories of crime in the upper 25%. The box plot also indicates where there might be outliers. Outliers are cases which are very different from the rest of the cases. They are shown here by circles and stars. In our example, the stalking and harassment boxplot shows an outlier.

Exploring your data through descriptive statistics and graphical presentation as shown in this chapter can enable you to make a judgement on the nature of your data in terms of its distribution, underlying patterns and structures. Therefore, you may consider descriptive statistics as the first step in quantitative analysis. As an exploratory tool, descriptive statistics can uncover hidden patterns in your data and help you decide on further analysis that may be needed.

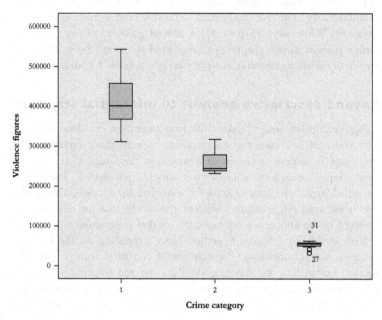

N.B. Crime category:

1= Violent crime with injury; 2 = Violent crime without injury; 3 = Stalking and harassment.

Figure 9.5 Boxplots of violent crime in England and Wales 2003–2015

Univariate, bivariate and multivariate analysis

As mentioned earlier it is important to make a distinction between different forms of analyses in relation to the number of variables involved. The example in the first case study is a case of univariate analysis where we deal with one variable – volume of crime in England and Wales. Although we are interested in different types of crime in the study, we are not looking for or attempting to compare crime variable with any other variable. In a bivariate analysis, the focus is to examine the relationships between two variables: the explanatory and the outcome variable. The explanatory variable is the variable which is thought to be the variable of influence (it is also known as the independent, input or predictor variable). The outcome variable (also known as the dependent variable) is the one that we believe will be affected by the explanatory variable.

In a multivariate analysis, you can analyse more than two variables simultaneously. The techniques used to do this kind of analysis are quite advanced. While we have provided a general guide to analysing multivariate analysis in this chapter, you may need to consult books that deal specifically with quantitative analysis (see recommended reading list).

Beyond descriptive analysis to inferential statistics

Using descriptive analysis, you will have described the data that you have collected and identified relationships between those variables. The next stage in analysis is to test to what extent the results of the data in your sample are generalisable to your sample's population. These tests are called hypothesis tests or tests for statistical significance. The results from these tests tell you how confident you can be that the relationships observed in the sample are representative of that population.

You would use different hypothesis tests depending on the types of variables you are analysing. For example, if you were dealing with categorical explanatory and outcome variables and you require a chi-square test of association, then Phi or Cramer's V test will be appropriate. See Appendix 2 for a list of statistical tests and a brief notes on what they are designed to measure.

All of these tests will carry with them certain assumptions about your data. For example, they might require that your data be normally distributed, independent, continuous. However, in terms of hypothesis testing there is one assumption that is extremely important. The data needs to have been drawn from a random sample. Hypothesis tests are carried out when you want to know whether something found is a quirk of the data set or something that is a feature of the population.

A test carried out on a non-random sample cannot speak with confidence about generalising to the population. If your sample is not random, you would be advised to spend your time carrying out a thorough descriptive analysis and trying to interpret what is happening in the sample that you have collected. If you collect your own data for your undergraduate dissertation, you are unlikely to have a truly random sample large enough to analyse with inferential statistics. For this reason, we will not go too deep into inferential statistics in this book. If you are working with a random sample (if you are analysing data that has been collected by someone else as part of a much bigger survey, for example), you may look at some of the books in the list at the end of this chapter that will introduce you to some of the more sophisticated statistical techniques. You may also need to discuss analysis options with your dissertation supervisor.

Analysing relationships – inferential statistics and hypothesis testing

Inferential statistics involves testing hypotheses in relation to the type of relationship that exist between variables. Part of this may involve measuring the degree of correlation.

Measuring correlation

Correlation is a statistical method for uncovering the nature and strength of relationships, if any, that exist between two or more variables. Not only will this technique tell you the kind of relationship that exists, but also enables you to evaluate, through hypothesis testing, the statistical validity of your result based on your sample data. You can carry out calculations to assess the degree or extent your two variables are related. The degree or association or correlation is determined by calculating the 'correlation coefficients', and they are usually a value between zero and one.

Relationships between two events, or variables X and Y, could be described in two ways:

- We could have an association between two variables where there is some kind of influence of one variable on the other, i.e. how X influences Y and vice versa;
- We could have a case of a causal relationship where one variable X causes change to occur in the other variable Y.

A causal link exists if changes in event X triggers an action or reaction in event Y. This is often referred to as a 'cause and effect' relationship. The cause is often referred to as the independent variable; the variable that is affected is known as the dependent variable.

The correlation between two events or variables X and Y can be described as:

- None (no correlation) – where changes in X has no effect on Y and vice versa;
- Positive (positive correlation) – where an increase in one variable results in an increase in the other variable, or a decrease in one variable results in a decrease in the other variable);
- Negative (negative correlation) – where an increase in one variable generates a decrease in the other.

Here are two common correlation coefficients:

- *Pearson's r.* This measures the relationship between two continuous variables. The value ranges from -1 (a perfect negative relationship) through 0 (no relationship) to +1 (perfect positive relationship). In order to conduct a Pearson's r test, your data needs to meet certain assumptions:

  (*a*) The two variables need to have a normal distribution (i.e. the histogram would look like an upside-down bell); and
  (*b*) When the variables are plotted against each other in a scatterplot, there needs to be a linear relationship between them.

- *Spearman's rho.* This test is similar to *Pearson's r* but your data do not need to meet the same assumptions. In this test, variables are ranked. A ranking of +1 shows a perfect relationship. It is possible to use Spearman's rho with both continuous and categorical data.

Case study 9.2 Analysing relationships using socio-economic deprivation and crime data for English towns and cities 2015

Problem definition

A researcher interested in housing and socio-economic deprivation in English towns and cities obtained the data shown in Appendix 2. The objective of the study is to establish any connection between the degree of deprivation and crime in selected towns/cities using appropriate statistical analysis.

(**Data Source:** Office for National Statistics licensed under the Open Government Licence.)

In order to test for statistical validity of any connection between deprivation and crime, the following hypotheses were posed:

The Null Hypothesis H_0:

There is no statistically significant relationship between level of deprivation and crime rates in English towns and cities.

The Alternative Hypothesis H_1:

There is a statistically relationship/connection between level of deprivation and crime rates in English towns and cities.

Given that the data set is ranked, it is appropriate to use *Spearman's rho* correlation technique to test whether or not there is a relationship between deprivation and crime and if any such relationship is statistically significant at 95% level of confidence. Tips for IBM-SPSS procedure for *Spearman's rho* correlation analysis:

- Log on and enter your data into IBM-SPSS.
- Define your variables, e.g. index of multiple deprivation rank (IMD) and crime rank figures.
- Analyse menu.
- Correlation statistics.
- Correlate > bivariate.
- Move the two variables into the variable list box, e.g. IMD Rank and Crime Rank.
- Select the appropriate correlation method e.g. Spearman.
- Select the required test of significance, e.g. 2-tailed.
- Check flag significant correlations box.
- Click OK.

Tips for IBM-SPSS procedure for scatter plots and fitting regression line

- From graphs menu, select scatter.
- Choose simple scatterplot and click on define button.
- Move the Crime Rank variable into the Y-axis box.
- Move the IMD variable into the X-axis box.
- Click on OK.
- Double click the graph to open the chart editor.
- Under chart menu, select options.
- Check fit line box.
- Check Display R-Square in legend.
- Check include constant in equation.
- Click continue.
- Click OK.

Results:

The result shows that there is a strong connection between level of deprivation and level of crime in English towns and cities (See Table 9.6 and Figure 9.5).

Table 9.6   Correlation matrix of index of multiple deprivation (IMD) and level
of crime in English towns and cities

Correlations

			Index of multiple deprivation	Crime
Spearman's rho	Index of multiple deprivation	Correlation Coefficient	1.000	.687**
		Sig. (2-tailed)	.	.000
		N	109	109
	Crime	Correlation Coefficient	.687**	1.000
		Sig. (2-tailed)	.000	.
		N	109	109

** . Correlation is significant at the 0.01 level (2-tailed).
Source: IBM-SPSS Spearman Correlation, derived from **Socio-economic deprivation in English towns and cities – 2015, Office of National Statistics.**

Hypothesis testing offers the opportunity to establish whether there is strong enough evidence in the sample of data that you collected to infer or make a judgement on whether certain condition is true or false for the entire population to which your data relate. This is based on the nature and strength of connection between two variables (bivariate analysis). Inferential statistics require an understanding of key statistical concepts such as hypothesis formulation, correlation, cross-tabulation, bivariate analysis, confidence interval and statistical significance.

Figure 9.6 shows the scatterplots of index of multiple deprivation and crime based on the data in our case study.

In this example the relationship between the two variables is positive since an increase in the value of one variable show an increase in the other. The figure suggests a positive connection between crime and deprivation rank in English towns and cities.

Crime and deprivation – regression line

The line that runs through the middle of the scatter points in Figure 9.6 is known as the regression line. A relationship between two

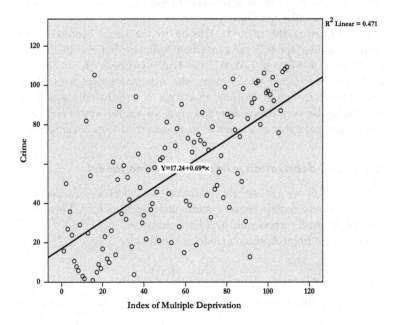

Figure 9.6 Scatterplots of index of multiple deprivation and crime in English towns and cities

quantitative variables that can be represented by a straight line is called a linear relationship. One of the objectives of simple linear regression analysis is to help us determine the best line through the data points in a scatterplot. One common way of determining this line is through the method of least squares; therefore, the regression line is also known as the least square line. The underlying principle of the least square method is that the line of best fit through the scatter is such that the sum of the squares of the deviations from the points to the line is minimum. While a correlation statistic shows how closely the data points are distributed around a straight line, regression analysis involves calculating and fitting a line of best fit across the middle of the data points.

While the scatterplot provides a visual picture as to the nature of relationships between the two variables, Table 9.6 gives a much more detailed statistic with a correlation coefficient of 0.687 and significance level, p of 0.000. This means there is a strong positive correlation between crime and level of deprivation in our case study and the correlation is statistically significant.

In interpreting the result in relation to the stated hypotheses, we need to consider not only the correlation coefficient but also the level of significance, p. Since $p < 0.01$, the Null hypothesis H_o in our case study can be rejected which means the Alternative hypothesis H_1 is true. Therefore, we can conclude that there is a statistically significant relationship between deprivation and crime in English towns and cities and we can make that conclusion at more than 99% level of confidence.

Crime and deprivation – linear regression model

In Figure 9.6, we can see the mathematical model or equation that defines the relationship between crime and deprivation. A linear relationship is usually represented by a linear equation.

The simple linear regression model is stated as:

$$Y = a + bx + e$$

Where Y is the dependent (or predicted) variable; (in our example – crime)

   a is the intercept (the point at which the regression line touches the Y-axis)

   x is the independent (or predictor) variable (IMD)

   b is the slope or gradient of the regression line

   e is the error term (that is the stochastic disturbance or the residuals).

Therefore, the mathematical model or equation that defines the relationship between crime and deprivation in English towns and cities can be stated as:

$$Y = 17.24 + 0.59 * X.$$

The R-Square value of 0.471 suggests that 47.1% of the variations in crime in English towns and cities can be explained by the level of multiple deprivation in those cities and towns.

Multivariate analysis and advanced analytical techniques

In our case study 9.2, we used only one explanatory variable, index of multiple deprivation (IMD) to explain the dependent variable (crime). You can use more than one independent variable to explain variations in crime. For example, the technique of multiple linear regression will enable you to use two or more explanatory variables in your analysis. You can learn more about multiple linear regression and other advanced statistical from relevant textbooks.

To help you along, we've included a number of variables in Appendix 2 that could help you with this. For example, you may wish to explore the relationship between crime and income deprivation, employment deprivation, health deprivation, education, skills and training deprivation, barriers to housing services and living environment deprivation. Using advanced statistical technique, you can determine the extent to which each of the factors listed above contribute to crime level in English towns and cities and the joint contribution of all the factors to the problem of crime in English towns and cities.

Besides multiple linear regression, there are a number of other advanced statistical and analytical techniques that are used in social sciences, such as modelling, hierarchical structure analysis, multinomial logistic techniques, factor analysis, etc., that are beyond the level expected of an undergraduate study. If you are thinking of doing postgraduate studies, it may well be that you are interested in developing your analytical skills further in these areas.

Data interpretation

The data analytical techniques described above offer you ways to summarise, describe and compare your data. Importantly, however, you will still need to interpret that data by asking yourself the question – what is the data trying to tell me? You should return to your initial hypothesis, research question or theory and see whether your data supports them. You need to explain why the data are saying what they are saying. In order to do this, you will need to draw on your knowledge of the topic area (gained from your reading) and also your reflection on your research approach. For example, were there limitations to your study that may have resulted in certain findings? Your interpretation should show how your research has extended, confirmed or confounded understandings of the social world. A tip regarding data analysis would be not to attempt to analyse too much data. Pick a shorter time span, a smaller population or maybe fewer indices. Using up a lot of time on data analysis is not always productive.

Key messages

- You need to understand the data that you are working with so that any calculations that you perform are valid.
- Descriptive analysis allows you to examine the variables you have in your data set and to establish relationships between them.
- There is no point conducting tests to establish the generalisability of your findings if you have a small sample, collected through convenience sampling.
- If you are carrying out analysis of an existing data set, techniques of inferential statistics might well be appropriate.
- Investigate computer packages that will help you with your analysis – investment of time in learning the software will pay dividends in terms of time spent analysing the data.

Key questions

- Does your university support a data analysis package and have you identified a package that can help you?
- Do you know which variables you are working with?
- Have you described your data using the appropriate techniques?
- Have you used the right checks to establish relationships between your variables?
- Does your sample comply with the assumptions necessary to carry out tests of statistical significance?
- Have you allowed enough time to interpret your statistics?

Further reading

Bryman, A. and Cramer, D. (1994). *Quantitative Data Analysis for Social Scientists*. London: Routledge.

Field, A. (2014). *Discovering Statistics Using IBM SPSS Statistics* (5th Edition). London: Sage.

Leech, N. L.; Barrett, K. C. and Morgan, G. A. (Eds) (2015). *IBM SPSS for Intermediate Statistics: Use and Interpretation* (5th Edition), New York and London: Routledge.

Pallant, J. (2016). *SPSS Survival Manual*. Berkshire: McGrawHill.

Shapiro, T. (2015). *Statistics for Political Analysis*. London: Sage.

Chapter 10

Analysing qualitative data

Introduction

This chapter focuses on how to analyse non-numeric data such as interviews, focus groups, surveys, talk, text and visual data. These data include written, printed or web texts, transcripts of spoken words, field notes from observations, research memos and also images (Fairclough 2003: 3). While there are a range of data sources falling under the umbrella of 'qualitative data', similarly there are a range of strategies available to analyse the data. There is, however, no singularly correct way to carry out qualitative data analysis and you will need to spend time choosing an approach that suits you. Qualitative data analysis is time-consuming, interpretative and iterative; it involves close attention to detail and good organisational skills. The chapter explains how computer software, such as NVivo, can be used as a tool to help you analyse your qualitative data.

By the end of this chapter, you should have a better understanding of:

- Preparing your data for qualitative analysis
- Different methods or ways of analysing qualitative data
- Computer software packages to aid your qualitative data analysis
- Specific approaches to qualitative data analysis, through case study and example
- How to assess the quality of your qualitative data analysis.

Preparing data for analysis

You might be lucky enough to have data in a form which is ready to analyse, for example, documents in electronic form that you can manipulate. Most qualitative data, however, comprise written notes (perhaps scribbled during field observations or interviews), audio files and visual data. The process of getting information, comprising spoken words, ideas, thoughts, speeches, etc., into a written or printed form is generally referred to as transcribing.

Most audio recordings of interviews will need to be transcribed. The amount of the raw data to transcribe will depend on the purpose of your interview. While some transcriptions only capture a summary of the main points of an interview, for example, others may need a full and verbatim transcriptions. If your aim is to gather factual information from your recorded interview, you may be selective in what you choose to transcribe. In which case, a few extracts from your recorded interview as quotes may be sufficient. If, however, you are interested in the structure of your respondents' arguments in order to know the implied meanings of their words, then you may need an extensive transcript. The most commonly used approach is verbatim transcription (Figure 10.1). This is where you note who said what and what they said. It is important that you remove any identifying features from the transcripts (such as names, addresses and other personal data). See Chapter 8 for ethics and law regarding handling personal data.

In your transcription, you might tidy up the language so that all the conversational fillers such as 'erm' are removed, but equally you might leave them in. If you are doing conversational or discourse analysis, you are probably going to want to have more detail in your transcript, including markers of stress, intonation and changes in pitch or volume. Transcription is time-consuming, so it is essential you leave enough time to transcribe your data. The more detailed your recording, the longer it will take to transcribe. Whichever method of transcription you use, it is important to ensure the accuracy and integrity of the information is maintained and you are able to check your transcription against the original data to ensure there is no loss of critical information during transcription.

Although it seems like a long and tedious task, transcribing your own data gives you a head start with your data analysis because you will become very familiar with it. It is good practice to duplicate your original data or recordings used in qualitative analysis and to catalogue or index each piece of information with a unique serial number for reference purposes.

Phases in qualitative data analysis

In an article written for 'rookie' qualitative researchers, Baptiste (2001) outlines a framework which aims to help researchers new to qualitative data analysis see the common features of qualitative data analysis. The paper was

46	I	So what kind of things do they need then, this group particularly?
47	R	Well, I think, um, in terms (...) uh, th-the/?/it's partly an issue you know, kind
48		of about what we set up for them in terms of the teaching. So if weh—
49	I	Yeah.
50	R	.../educationally/, I mean so much of our teaching to data has been geared
51		toward maturer applicants who may be have more experience of the practice of
52		social work. so we're having to think more actively about, about how to, to
53		manage our teaching so that it copes, it is appropriate to both groups of
54		Students.
55	I	Right, yeah.
56	R	Um...er, you know, so that we're not completely talking over the heads of the
57		new students in terms of these, and the king of historical things that we're
58		talking about, let alone the kind of intellectual ones.
59	I	Yeah, yeah.
60	R	Um, so so there's that. For those students, I, and yeah, I suppose in that
61		regard you know, one of the things that, which is not exactly answering your
62		que-, not directly answering your question, but it's sort of indicative of what
63		we've identifid/as needs/, is that within the last, within this last year we have
64		specifically developed a, um, a special set of activities, really, opportunities for
65		those groups of students to go and just explore—
66	I	Right.
67	R	...different social work and social care agencies, you know, ouve and above the
68		opportunities that students would ordin-, ordinarily have. You know, because
69		that helps give them a bit more grounding in what's being talked about.
70	I	Yeah.
71	R	So that's the academics, you know, the subject support thing.
72	I	Yeah.
73	R	Um, I think that um socially um you know those students. h-um (...) you know
74		ther-, as I say, you know, kind of numbers on board living away from home for
75		the first time, there's, there's not a lot, that won't be true for all of them, you
76		know, but um, and dealing with the social challenges of living in halls, which has
77		you know pros ans cons to it, I suppose. you can feel very isolated as well as
78		very together with people in those kinds of settings I think.
79	I	Yeah, yeah.

Figure 10.1 Extract from a verbatim transcript

written because he found that his students were bewildered by the multitude of approaches to qualitative data analysis. He outlines four phases:

1. Defining the analysis
2. Classifying the data
3. Making connections between and among categories of data
4. Conveying the message or the write-up.

The key stages and phases in qualitative data analysis are summarised in Figure 10.2. The stages may not necessarily follow a linear chronological

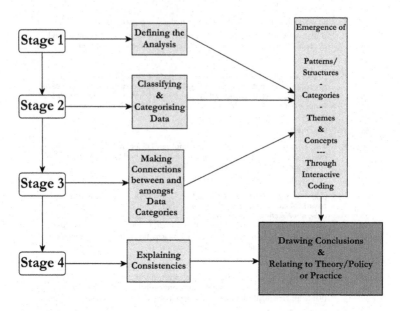

Figure 10.2 Stages in qualitative data analysis

order as it is often necessary to revisit or review actions in previous phase to improve the reliability of your qualitative research.

Defining the analysis

This first phase is as much a part of your research design as it is a part of data analysis, further highlighting the point that design, data collection and data analysis are inextricably linked – especially in qualitative research.

The approach adopted for your qualitative data analysis is often dependent on what you consider to be valued as knowledge: your *epistemology*. The epistemological questions that you ask yourself relate to how you would try to acquire knowledge, what you believe counts as knowledge and how you would know (Baptiste 2001). You should also consider what you deem to be real: your *ontology*. When we think about ontological positions, we need to be clear about what we see as real and how our understanding of reality shapes how we do our research (Baptiste 2001). A further consideration is around the values and ethics associated with your approach to your research: your *axiology*. You need to consider to what extent your values will impact on your analysis, the role that your research participants will play in your research and what you will then do with the output of your research. The main factors to consider while choosing your qualitative data analysis approach are shown in Figure 10.3.

It may seem that this section is encouraging you to ask some very hard and deeply philosophical questions about your research: that is the aim. Qualitative analysis, by nature, is interpretive, and your epistemological, ontological and axiological positions will inevitably influence your methodology and subsequently your approach to analysis. It is therefore important for you to be able to articulate your position and to be able to evaluate the impact that position will have on your research – particularly its strengths and limitations.

Classifying the data

In the second phase, you begin the process of classifying your data. Becoming familiar with that data is one of your first priorities. Before you formally begin your analysis, you should allocate some time to briefly look through and read the data collected. This will include listening to the recordings of any interviews and reading through the transcripts, looking at the notes you wrote for yourself during the data collection period, and watching any video footage that you have. As you go through this cycle of reading and rereading, you will already be starting to notice patterns and similarities in your data. You are beginning to develop a template for conducting the full analysis. Analysing qualitative data is very time-consuming. You may need to go back over transcripts when new ideas occurred to you. So, make sure you leave enough time to do that. Analysis isn't about reporting what your participants say – it's about what they mean. You need to try and move beyond just describing your data to actually understanding your participants' views and thoughts on the issue or subject of investigation.

Coding your data

Having classified your data, the next step is to further develop the template through coding. The process of coding involves picking out the bits of your data set that you think are interesting and useful for the research that you are carrying out. The criteria for assigning codes to your data may be based on the topic, story, event, signifiers, idea,

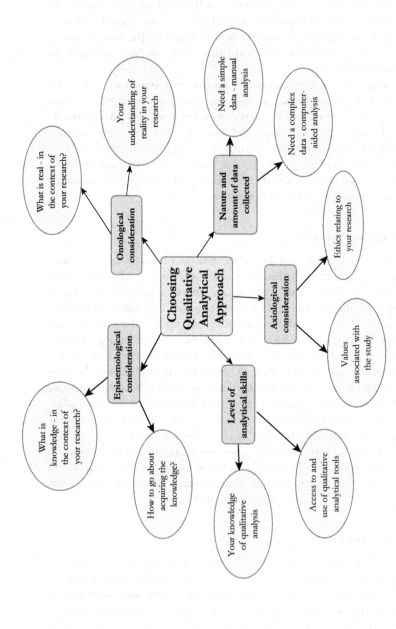

Figure 10.3 Factors to consider in choosing qualitative data analysis technique

theme, concept or theory relating to or suggested by your data. You can code your data deductively. i.e. based on your pre-existing idea, hunches or theories about what you think the data may be showing or what you considered important within the data or inductively, based on emerging issues or patterns within the data (Neale 2016). You may find that the notes you made while collecting your data could be developed into codes or labels. The same codes might come up frequently; you can then read through the data set and highlight every time that the code is represented. You can choose to use the actual words that are used in your data set as your labels – this is called 'in-vivo coding' – or you can choose to name them yourself. If you prefer, it is also possible to analyse your data more deductively. In which case the template you are using is pre-defined and not emergent. That means that you will go into the data set to look for specific concepts which match your pre-defined codes before you start your analysis. Whichever method you choose will, invariably, be influenced by your experience and the literature you have read. You may even decide to combine both inductive and deductive coding. Figure 10.4 shows possible criteria for assigning labels or codes to your data.

Once you are happy with your coding scheme, there are different ways that you can mark your codes. You may choose to make notes of key words in the margin of your transcript. Alternatively, you might prefer to get out your highlighter pens and to mark up the codes in different colours. You will find that some pieces of data will relate to more than one code, so you need to be sure that the method you have adopted can cater for these overlaps. The important point is that you find a method that works for you. Figure 10.5 shows a transcript which is in the process of being annotated.

As you work through the data identifying codes and highlighting them, you may begin to suffer from 'code overload'. At this point, you need to stand back and see whether you are using different codes to describe the same thing. If you are, then you should see whether only one code can be used instead. This type of pruning the codes used throughout analysis will be ongoing. Having coded all of your data, you can now start to look for ways to connect those codes together into themes, concepts or categories. As you do this, you should be checking whether these themes are distinct from each other and that you have sufficient data to support each of them. You should be willing to redefine the categories as you go deeper into your analysis.

In order to do this grouping, you may decide to cut up a printed version of your transcripts and cluster your codes together into different categories. The beauty of this approach is that you can keep

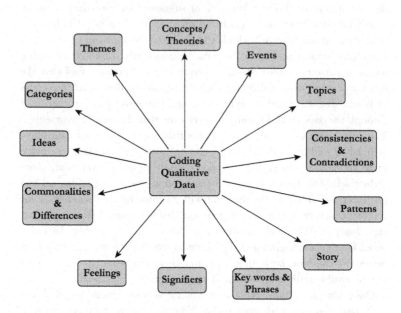

Figure 10.4 Assigning codes and labels to your qualitative data

moving the pieces around until you find the most suitable home for them. You could use the cut and paste function in your word-processing package to copy fragments of your data into a document named after the theme. When you do this, keep the contextual detail of your extracts (e.g. which transcript or which set of field notes the data came from). It is important that you can reference where your materials come from. If you are systematic here, it will save you a lot of time later down the line. If not, time will be wasted searching for individual quotes. You might, for example, choose to display your categories diagrammatically through concept maps or spider diagrams, as shown in Figure 10.6. As with coding, you need to find a method which allows you to see the connections between your data more clearly. Following a successful coding and data classification, analysis becomes more creative and more interesting and the next stage is making connections.

Making connections

In this phase, the aim is to help you and your readers to understand more deeply and more broadly the area investigated. As you interpret your findings, you will be looking for connections between the categories

1 (I) But you did alright didn't you? you got a good mark
2 (R) Yeah yeah
3 (I) Yeah? So what do yoy think? I mean you got a 2:1 and yoy sat you just, you
4 know, just did enough. Yet what strategies did you use then in order to get that I mean
5 cos you could easily have got a 2:2 couldn't you, with that?
6 (R) Yeah
7 (I) Approach but you got a 2:1. What do you think you learned, in terms of working in
8 academia that got you the 2:1 and not a 2:2?
9 (R) Basically I knew how to like balance my life, like the social aspect of it,
10 and I knew when to study ⎯⎯ Strategy
11 (I) OK, so you could, like, if you had an exam coming up you would-
12 (R) Yeah definitely. And when I was studying my undergrad I was like so far away
13 from homw and I was thinking well I've come all this way I don't want to go home,
14 you know, disappointing my family, cos what was the point in me going all this way
15 if I was going to do home and fail.
16 (I) Yep
17 (R) So that was always playing at the back of my mind ⎯⎯ worried him
18 (I) OK so there was that pushing you, yep, ok. So coming into this course then. Do you
19 think that there are any particular skills that you needed in order to do well on this
20 module?   ☆
21 (R) I think like the past four years I've lacked in confidence, so one of the reasons was
22 to gain in confidence cos I just felt you know I was you know like useless in life cos
23 I'd not like made really much use out of my first degree
24 (I) Yep
25 (R) So I just come here to like build up my confidence, mainly ⎯ Build person
26 (I) Yep. Do you think that this module has helped you do that?
27 (R) Yes but I feel as though I didn't help myself by participating more in group work
28 (I)OK.   /
                                    Not pushed himself

Figure 10.5 **Example of a coded extract**

that you have identified. What are the relationships between those categories? Are they of equal importance? Are there sociological theories
that could help to interpret what is happening in the data? What does
the literature say about the area you are researching and how do your
own findings compare? The key issue is being able to show how the
findings from your study relate to findings from other studies, thus
deepening our understanding of the area you are researching.

Using software for qualitative data analysis

The method that has been described in previous sections describes
a process that you can carry out without any particular data analysis software. It involves very basic techniques: coloured pens, scissors, glue,
pencils, a word-processing package and multiple copies of transcripts.
This is a manual approach to data analysis. As with quantitative data

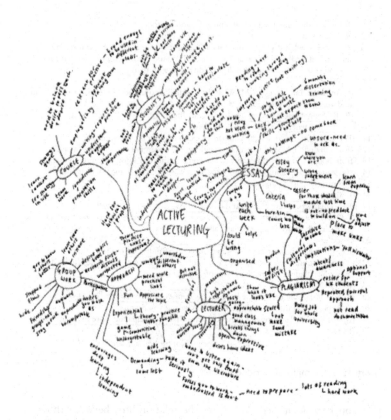

Figure 10.6 Example of a mind map (for you to view, not to read)

analysis, there are software packages which can be used to help you manage the analysis. The tools these packages offer can help to organise, manage, search and code your data set. You need to remember, though, that they can only help your analysis – they will not do it for you. Deep engagement with the data will still involve you doing the thinking, and no computer package can do that for you.

One of the greatest benefits of qualitative data analysis packages is their data management functions. This means that they come into their own if you are working with large and complicated data sets. If you have never used qualitative data analysis software before and you are working with a small data set, you should ask yourself whether it is worth taking the time out of your dissertation to learn a package and what the advantages would be in doing so. If you've used qualitative data analysis packages before, if your institution has a licence for them, or if you hope to do more qualitative research in the future then there might be good reasons to give computer-aided analysis a try.

Most computer packages designed to analyse qualitative data are able to support data management, coding and searching. Many are now able to deal with different types of data, including, for example, audio, visual and textual data. Nine commonly used computer-aided qualitative data analysis packages are:

ATLAS.ti
QDA Miner
Tams Analyzer
Dedoose
NVivo
MAXQDA
HyperRESEARCH
Aquad
Transana

While you may have access to a number of the packages listed above, most universities will hold a licence for the software NVivo which is a popular qualitative data analysis tool. As such, in the following section we have offered a general guide to NVivo, but make sure you check with your own institution prior to planning your analysis. It is highly unlikely that you will not receive guidance, classes or worksheets on data analysis from your own institution. As such the information provided only offers a simple introduction to the programme, and you may need to consult relevant texts and institution guides to learn more about the software.

Using NVivo for analysing your data

NVivo allows you to organise, sort and manage non-numerical data. It can enable you to analyse and handle data in an effective way that you may not otherwise be able to do manually. NVivo is particularly useful in organising and analysing a large volume of data. With NVivo, it is easier to locate common patterns or structures from within your data. Those patterns or common topic identified within your data are stored as *Nodes* in NVivo. The software can handle a variety of non-numerical data including video recordings, word documents and field notes. The main purpose of the application is to identify relationships between your data and to record any discernible patterns. You can also use the programme to summarise your data using charts, models and other visual formats.

Apart from ensuring a systematic analysis of your data, NVivo can also be used in managing your literature review and other documents and resources used in your dissertation. The programme enables you to import texts, documents, pictures and other materials including PDF document, journals, PowerPoints, and audio recordings for your analysis. It uses a systematic coding processes to generate themes, common topics, and relationships within your documents. This may be useful if you want to identify common themes in literature in order to formulate your research questions. You can also use the programme to test or verify hypotheses and it allows you to ask specific questions relating to your data, using its 'query' tools. The programme can also help you in drawing conclusions from your data based on your literature review and data analysis.

Other approaches to qualitative data analysis

So far, we have described a very general approach to qualitative data analysis, which could loosely be described as thematic analysis. We have outlined a process of coding, categorisation, theme development and comparison. This can be done manually or with the help of software packages.

There are, however, many other approaches to analysing qualitative data that we think you need to know about. Figure 10.7 shows the most common techniques for analysing qualitative data. Denzin and Lincoln's *The Sage Book of Qualitative Research* (2011) offers a comprehensive overview. Here we will focus on only some of them. This overview is not comprehensive but aims to give a feeling for some of the approaches that could be adopted.

Discourse analysis

Discourse analysis does not refer to one single approach; rather, it is a general term for approaches to the analysis of both written and spoken text. Different approaches to discourse analysis have grown out of different disciplines: linguistics, cognitive psychology and post-structuralism (Potter 2004: 201). Miller and Brewer (2003: 75–76) offer five broad categories of discourse analysis. The first is linguistic in focus and looks at discourse styles in social settings

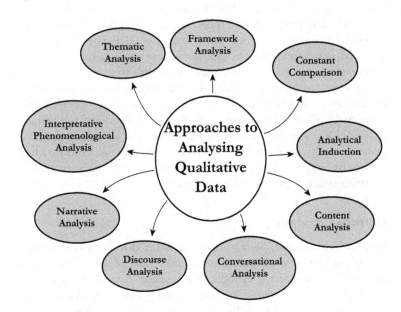

Figure 10.7 Qualitative analysis techniques

(such as school interactions, courtrooms, doctors' surgeries). The second looks at how language is used in natural situations – the *ethnography of communication* and the competencies needed for that communication. The third category, *conversation analysis*, investigates how conversation is organised. The fourth focuses on the choice of words used in the textual and verbal accounts of social representatives. The fifth, *critical discourse analysis*, sees language as being bound up with power and ideology; analysis focuses on how language benefits certain groups over others.

These approaches all have different emphases, yet they all share the understanding that language is a social act that is embedded within a social context which both influences and is influenced by language (Gee 2005).

Grounded theory

Grounded theory (Glaser and Strauss 1967) aims to develop theory out of the data which has been collected. This is different to many approaches to research where a theoretical framework is chosen at the beginning of a project and then the data analysed in relation to that framework. The process of data collection, data analysis and theory generation in grounded theory are closely connected. The research question is set and sample selected. The data is collected and coded, and concepts are generated. The coding shows where more data needs to be collected. This process continues until there is saturation (that is, no more codes are emerging). Relationships between the categories are identified and a theory postulated. This substantive theory is then tested in different settings. This may lead to the development of a formal theory. The grounded theory approach is not linear as it has been described here but is iterative and based on constant comparison, with different phases occurring simultaneously and being repeated.

Narrative analysis

Narrative analysis describes a suite of approaches that focuses on the analysis of the stories which people use to make sense of what Ezzy (2002) describes as disconnected episodes that together form a coherent construction of the past. The stories that narrative analysis analyses are the products of people who are living in a particular social, historical and cultural context; the stories they tell are a reflection of how they see themselves and others within their worlds (Lawler 2002). Narratives can be, among other things, used to give information, to structure our ideas about ourselves and to pass on experiences (Gibbs 2007: 60). Key examples of narratives are biographical and life-history accounts. There is little consensus on what narrative analysis involves, and Riessman has identified four different models (described in Bryman 2004: 412):

1. Thematic (focus on what is said)
2. Structural (focus on how it is said)
3. Interactional (focus on the dialogue between teller and listener)
4. Performative (focus on how the narrative is enacted).

Visual analysis

Visual analysis is used to analyse images which are both generated for the research study and those which are already in existence. Images can be 'researcher found' (generated by others) or 'researcher generated' (created by the researcher). Both are integral to the visual research process (Prosser 2006: 3). These images can be used as either aides-memoires or as data in their own right (Bryman 2004: 312). Most analytical approaches that are used for non-image-based research can also be used for those which involve images (Banks 2007: 38). A researcher analysing images needs to be sensitive to the context in which they were generated, the potential for multiple meanings and the impact of their own role in production of the images (Bryman 2004; Banks 2007). There are approaches to analysis which may be particularly appropriate to the analysis of visual images, for example:

- Semiotics – the study of signs and symbols to uncover their deeper meaning and how that meaning is understood (Chandler 1994)
- Qualitative content analysis – finding underlying themes in the images being analysed and situating those findings within the context in which the images were produced
- Ethnomethodological approaches – identifying the everyday practices by which people organise their lives (Banks 2007: 49).

These brief overviews of different approaches to data analysis have been designed to give you a taste of ways you can work with your data. If you choose to work with one of them, take a look at the recommended texts and also try and read a research paper which has adopted the same approach to analysis. This will show the ways in which the data analysis can be reported.

Checks on quality

In both quantitative and qualitative approaches, it is important to ensure that any analysis of data can produce information which can withstand questions around rigour and transparency. The quality control measures employed to scrutinise and check qualitative data will be different to those measures employed to assure quantitative analysis and there are checklists and guidelines available specifically for writing up qualitative research. Examples of such checklists and guidelines are as provided by Critical Appraisal Skills Programme (CASP 2013) and Consolidated Criteria for Reporting Qualitative Research (COREQ) (Tong et al. 2007).

In your research project, you want to be sure that your analysis is trustworthy. Miles and Huberman (1994: 277–280) offer five areas that you could use to assess the quality of your work.

1. *Objectivity/confirmability.* Is the study relatively objective? Have the researcher's biases been acknowledged?
2. *Reliability/dependability/auditability.* Was the approach to the study consistent and stable over time?

3. *Internal validity/credibility/authenticity.* Do the findings make sense? Are they credible? Do they paint a true picture of what we were studying?
4. *External validity/transferability/fittingness.* How do these findings fit into the bigger picture? Can they be generalised to other settings?
5. *Utilisation/application/action orientation.* What impact does the study have on the researchers and the researched? (Figure 10.8)

For each of the areas above, Miles and Huberman offer a series of questions that could form the basis of reflection on your study and, therefore, a check on its quality.

Key messages

- There is no single approach and no 'right way' to do qualitative data analysis.
- Many approaches share four general phases: analysis definition, data classification, connection-making and message conveyance.
- Analysis involves interpretation – establishing links to theory, literature and experiences.
- Software packages such as NVivo can aid your qualitative analysis.
- Any approach to data analysis needs to undergo checks on quality.

Figure 10.8 Capturing a Telling Instance

Key questions

• Have you researched different approaches to qualitative data analysis? Do you understand what differentiates them?
• Are you able to justify why your chosen approach to data analysis is appropriate in terms of the data you have collected and also your view of research?
• Have you adopted a systematic approach to data classification? Have you been through the classification cycle more than once?
• Have you sufficiently interpreted and explained patterns, categories and themes in your data? How do your findings fit with other work that is out there?
• Have you reflected honestly on your approach to data analysis? Where are the weaknesses and the strengths in what you have produced?

Further reading

Creswell, J. W. and Poth, C. N. (2018). *Qualitative Inquiry and Research Design: Choosing among Five Approaches* (4th Edition). London: Sage.

Denzin, N. K. and Lincoln, Y. S. (2018). *The Sage Handbook of Qualitative Research* (5th Edition). London: Sage.

Jackson, K. and Bazeley, P. (2019). *Qualitative Data Analysis with Nvivo* (3rd Edition). London: Sage.

Ritchie, J., Lewis, J., Nicholls, C. M. and Ormston, R. (2014). *Qualitative Research Practice: A Guide for Social Science Students & Researchers* (2nd Edition). London: Sage.

Silverman, D. (2014). *Interpreting Qualitative Data* (5th Edition). London: Sage.

Chapter 11

Writing the dissertation

Introduction

This chapter sets out the essential guidelines for writing your dissertation. The chapter provides key information on what makes a good dissertation and how you can make the most of the data you have collected. By the time you start to write the first draft of your dissertation, you will probably already have accumulated a wealth of notes, scribblings and ideas about what you want to write about. Your job, thereafter, is to put all those ideas and materials into a coherent structure. The importance of working with your supervisor's comments and proofreading are also highlighted in this chapter.

By the end of this chapter, you should have a better understanding of:

- How to get started on writing your dissertation
- Different parts of the dissertation and how to approach them
- How to prepare your dissertation for submission
- How our checklists can help ensure you have done all you need to do in writing a successful dissertation.

Drawing up a plan for writing your dissertation

It is highly advisable to draft a plan of the dissertation. There is a lot in common between different dissertations regarding the structure, and, although you do not need to stick slavishly to a standard plan, such a plan is very helpful as a template to impose some order on what may seem an unmanageable task. Splitting up the tasks into chapters, drawing up chapter plans and assigning a word count to each section may really help you with this initial planning.

Structuring your dissertation

The way you compose, write and present each of the component parts of your dissertation in terms of structure may vary from one study to another and depends on your institution's guidelines for dissertation. It is, therefore, important that you check the requirements for your institution. Browsing through past dissertations submitted to your institution by your predecessors may help you identify common structures. Most universities will have good examples of dissertations in the library that you may consult. You also need to pay attention to the style of presentation specified in your institution's guidelines, and other things such as the word limit (minimum and maximum), text fonts, text spacing style, etc.

A well-structured dissertation is usually logically presented and easy to read. The structure of your dissertation will depend, to a large extent, on your research aims and objectives. Although there is no single way of structuring a dissertation, most dissertations will comprise eleven parts:

- The title page
- Acknowledgements (if required)
- An abstract
- Contents page and figure/table lists
- Introduction section
- Methods and methodology section
- Literature review and theoretical/conceptual framework
- Analysis, findings and discussion of results section
- Conclusions
- References
- Appendices.

Title page

Your dissertation should have a clear title. The main title, including a subtitle if necessary, needs to reflect what the study is about and the contents of your dissertation. At an early stage, your title may be a provisional one, a 'working title', which you may need to revise or refine later. Your dissertation supervisor may advise on the title in order to help you find and define the focus of the dissertation. As your title says a lot about your study, it needs to be clear, succinct, specific and accurately describe your dissertation. Some institutions require that you indicate your full name on the title page with a statement on your course/programme of study, the name of your institution and your supervisor. For example,

A dissertation submitted in partial fulfilment of the requirements for the degree of BSc International Relations and Diplomacy, University of Derby, Kedleston Road, Derby, United Kingdom. Date Submitted: June 2019. Name of Supervisor: Dr Francis Jegede.

Writing and acknowledgements

Acknowledgements enable you to formally recognise and thank individuals, organisations or institutions that have helped you along the way on your dissertation journey. It is entirely up to you to decide who is worthy of mention in your acknowledgements. Many people may have helped you along the way – your supervisor, lecturers, parents, spouses or partners, your interviewees or participants, etc. You can get an idea of how to write your own by reading acknowledgements from other dissertations or books. Our own acknowledgements section at the beginning of this book also provides an example for you to follow.

Writing your abstract

An abstract is a short, but very important part of writing a dissertation. Also known as, 'resume' or 'executive summary' in some reports or documents, it is a brief summary of your dissertation. Usually about 300 words long, it highlights the purpose, methods of investigation, findings and conclusion of your study. A well written abstract will enable your reader to make a judgement on what your study is about and how relevant or interesting the study is. It is essentially an overview of your entire study. As it is a summary of everything about your study, it is usually the last section to write after all other sections and chapters have been written. Alternatively, you may decide to write your abstract earlier to help you identify key points or themes in your study that can help in the design of the structure of your dissertation. Your abstract is the first thing potential readers will read after your title page if you submit your dissertation to any publishing journal or research database. So, it's important to make a good impression!

Contents page and figure/table lists

The contents page provides a chronological order of contents of your dissertation. This can be manually created or auto-generated in Microsoft Word, if you apply the built-in heading styles to the headings and sub-headings in the texts of your dissertation. Similarly, figure/table lists contain a list of figures and tables in the order in which they appear in your dissertation.

Writing the introduction

The introduction may be the first chapter in your dissertation, but it does not have to be the first thing that you write. Your introduction should set the scene for your dissertation – what you want to do, how you want to do it and what you want to achieve doing it. Your study aims, objectives and rationale for your choice of techniques and methodology need to be made clear in this section. The main purpose of the introduction section is to provide the reader with the background and context to your research and to inspire an interest in your reader to want to read the rest of the dissertation. In this section, therefore, you need to explain the reason for choosing your dissertation topic, the key questions you set out to answer in your study and your motivation for undertaking the project. You should give the reader a clear understanding of the structure of your dissertation and key issues addressed in each chapter. It is necessary to split this into subsections, covering specific aspects such as:

- Background to the study
- Study aims and objectives
- Key research questions and hypotheses
- Structure of the dissertation.

It is useful to specify the significance and relevance of your study in this section.

Writing a literature review and linking your study to theories/concepts

The literature review section provides an opportunity to offer a critical overview of relevant past research relating to your dissertation. For full information on how to search and review literature, see Chapter 4. The literature review defines the context in which your research is situated and justifies why this is an important area to study. It is essential in this section to describe the current state of research relating to your study and consider other areas that may be closely related to your study. This allows you to synthesise current knowledge and identify any gap that your study is designed to fill. There are two parts to this section. The first is the review of literature and the second is reviewing specific theories or concepts that underpin your study. A well written literature review section will not only provide the theoretical and methodological context for your study, it could also explain the logic for your study aims and research design. It is advisable that you spend some time to ensure your literature review is comprehensive, critical, informative and relevant to your study, as you will refer back to this section in your discussion of findings section.

It is important to remember that a literature review is different to an annotated bibliography. An annotated bibliography lists the sources that you have identified and offers a summary of them one by one. A literature review, in contrast, will make comparisons between references, identify links and note developments in your subject area. There are different ways in which you can group the literature in your review. Three of the most common approaches include chronological, thematic and methodological.

- In a *chronologically organised* review, you order your review around the development through time of your area of interest.
- In a *thematically organised* review, the literature is presented around emergent issues or topics. Such a presentation of literature will highlight what the main themes are in your area of study. When conducting this kind of review, you will have to extract the key points from each source and look for connections with the other literature you have reviewed. The review will be presented through a series of sections and subsections.
- In *methodologically organised* reviews, the focus is on the methods used by the researcher to carry out his or her research rather than on the content of the research. Such a review will be appropriate if you are looking to develop knowledge about a method or an approach to research.

Whichever approach you adopt, you should see that the literature review ends by showing where your own research will add to the knowledge base in your area of interest. Organising your review chronologically, thematically or methodologically will also bring your empirical or theoretical work into sharper focus.

Writing the methods and methodology section

In the methodology section, you need to describe, explain and justify how and why you conducted the research in a particular way. It is important to be clear about things such as why you collected some data, why you chose a particular method of data collection or used any particular equipment, materials or processes. Your methodology section must be clear and detailed enough for anyone who may want to conduct similar study. Remember that in the methods section you are telling the reader what you did in your study. Since it is often straightforward to write, you might decide to do this chapter first. Since you are discussing something that has already happened, you should write this section in the *past tense*: for example, 'I interviewed eight people' or 'Eight people were interviewed' rather than 'I will interview eight people' or 'Eight people will be interviewed'.

The methods section must clearly identify the epistemological and ontological basis of the study and demonstrate a good working knowledge of the methods to be employed. It should include good coverage of the process of the fieldwork and indicate how the analysis was undertaken. As well as covering the ethical issues, it should also contain an element of reflection on the research process. At all stages, you should be making reference to research methods literature.

Here is a list of questions that you should ask yourself as you are writing the methods section:

- Have you stated your hypothesis or research questions clearly?
- Have you clearly outlined how you designed your research?
- Have you evaluated the type of data that you have collected?
- Have you evaluated and justified the method you have chosen?
- Have you explained the procedure you followed?
- Have you mentioned the equipment you used and the conditions under which you carried out your research?
- Have you described how you will analyse the data?

This is a critical section in your dissertation as it shows the research framework upon which your study is based.

Writing the findings and results section

There are different ways of presenting your research findings and writing your results. It is, therefore, important to follow your institution's guidelines before you write this section. You may also need to check which particular style of reporting is most suitable for your particular study. For example, you may want to make a clear distinction between the results and the discussion of those results, especially if you are writing a technical or a scientific dissertation. Alternatively, you may decide on having a 'Findings' section where you bring the results of your own analysis and your discussion of the results together in one place. Also, you can decide on the order of presentation of your results and whether to start from a generic overview and move on to specific findings, or vice versa, in reporting your findings.

Whichever approach you decide to use, it is important to understand the difference between findings and discussion. In the findings section, you are presenting what you have found in your research and what you interpret those findings to mean. The discussion section, however, is where you link your data analysis back to literature you introduced in your literature review. Some dissertation guidance will put the two together in one chapter, while others will ask for separate chapters. Make sure you check what is required at your institution. In your findings section, it is important that you present your results in a logical and convincing manner. If your results are presented in a confusing way, the reader will not follow your argument and may not trust your conclusions.

If you are presenting quantitative data, there are several things that you should consider. First, have you used the most appropriate way of presenting your data? Nominal data, for example, is best represented numerically by a frequency table and graphically by a pie chart; ordinal data often looks better with a bar chart representation; and for interval or ratio data, a frequency table will probably be very large, so a histogram would be better here. Whenever you introduce a table or chart into your dissertation, you need to ensure that this is clearly labelled with a title and a figure or table number. Make sure that all the data that you present is interpreted. It is not sufficient to just describe it. One common mistake that people make is that they merely repeat what is in the graphs in words. This is not interpretation, it is description. You also need to ensure that you refer to all the tables and charts somewhere in the text. If not, you need to ask yourself why those tables and charts are there.

When it comes to qualitative data, there are no fixed rules about the best way to present it. This means that you need to choose extracts from your data that evidence the arguments you are making in your data analysis. These can be, for example, quotes from your interviews or focus groups or notes or photographs from your observations. Quotes and other raw data will bring your analysis to life and will make your findings more credible. As with quantitative data analysis, you should clearly label your data extracts. Whether your results are quantitative, qualitative or a mixture of both, there are some things to bear in mind:

- Have you given a clear overview of what you have found out from your research?
- Have you included any data which are not needed?
- Have you interpreted your data and not just described it?
- Have you labelled all your tables, figures and quotes?

Writing the discussion section

The discussion section enables you to position your research within a wider context of existing knowledge in the subject or area of investigation. It is necessary to include in your discussion some information on how your research has contributed to our understanding of the subject or improved existing knowledge. The limitations of your study also need to be acknowledged and their implications for the validity of your results and your conclusion. The discussion section is particularly important and needs to be written carefully as it is the place where you show the significance of your findings and highlight what has been achieved when compared to your original aims. There are arguments for extending the coverage of literature in this section but only in exceptional circumstances, such as when you have obtained completely different results to what you expected. The discussion should be an opportunity to raise the different voices of interest in the research question and to explore the findings in the light of the literature and different perspectives within it.

Writing the conclusion

Compared to other sections in your dissertation, your conclusion should be relatively short but should contain a detailed summary of your research. In writing your conclusion, all the strands of your argument need to come together to give a convincing and forceful answer to the research question you set out to study. You also need to justify your conclusion and show how you arrive at the conclusion based on your data or information. You need to identify your key findings and policy or practice implications of those findings. Based on your conclusions, you may offer some recommendations. Apart from just being a summary section, your conclusion offers the opportunity to review your work as a whole, to identify the points of comparison and contrast the various texts you have examined, and to show that, in the process of your study, you have developed a more precise, critical understanding of the way they deal with your topic. This is also an appropriate place for you to point to the potential limitations of small-scale research of this kind and to reflect on possible avenues for researchers to address the issues in the future.

Compiling your list of references

After writing all your sections and noting all the sources you used for your dissertation, you need to compile a list of references. This should be structured and listed alphabetically by surnames of authors. You need to make sure that you utilise the referencing style that you prefer or that is prescribed by your institution. Whatever style you adopt, whether it be Harvard, Oscaola, APA or something else, it is important that you stick to one and are consistent in your referencing style throughout your dissertation. It is essential that you list all your references within the text of your dissertation and all sources cited in the text should be included in the list of references. Ensure that you cite your sources correctly to avoid being accused of the serious academic offence of plagiarism.

Acknowledging the work of others

In Western academic culture, there is the underlying belief that academic endeavour aims to build knowledge and that knowledge builds on knowledge already generated by others (through using that knowledge, borrowing it, modifying it or disregarding it). When producing new knowledge, it is understood that the originators of previous knowledge need to be recognised and acknowledged. If you do not do this and you use other people's ideas, words, thoughts or work without acknowledging them, then you are committing an academic offence known as plagiarism.

Appendices

Appendices is the section where you show materials that you want your readers to see but do not want to put in the main sections of your dissertation. This could be a sample questionnaire, letters of correspondence, the output of SPSS statistical analysis or full a transcript of an interview conducted. Since these documents often take up a lot of space, it is essential that you check whether the appendices count within the word limit for your dissertation. All appendices should be numbered in numerical order and listed in the table of contents.

Final draft

The process of preparing your dissertation for submission begins with a careful final reading of all your chapters and sections. Here you can:

- Ensure that your argument is clearly developed from sentence to sentence, from paragraph to paragraph and from chapter to chapter.
- Check the accuracy of your spelling and punctuation.
- Make sure that your sentences are well constructed and that you are expressing yourself clearly, precisely and fluently.
- Ensure that you have not contradicted or repeated yourself.
- Check whether your working title adequately describes the content of your dissertation or whether you need to change it.

You need to check that your quotations from and references to both primary and secondary texts are clearly and consistently identified according to the conventions of the referencing systems your institution requires. After completing your first draft, make sure you have covered all areas by checking again that:

- The title page shows the correct title, your name, the award and the date
- All the pages of the dissertation are correctly numbered
- The table of contents is correct and entries link to the correct page number in your dissertation
- There is consistency in terms of style and layout of your dissertation.

Proofreading

Your final task before you submit should be to proofread your dissertation. In this final stage, you will be looking for grammatical and typographical errors. At this point, you will have read your dissertation many times, so it will be very familiar to you. You, therefore, need to use strategies to help you see your dissertation through different eyes. If you have been drafting thus far on your computer, print out a copy of the dissertation as mistakes are often easier to spot when in print. Read your dissertation out loud and see whether what you are saying makes sense. You could also read through concentrating on the grammar and spelling rather than the content. Doing this makes you look at each word individually, rather than skim-reading.

When you have read through the whole dissertation, make any necessary changes and then go back to check the layout and presentation guidelines given by your institution to ensure that your dissertation is in the correct format. Then you can print the final document, and have it bound (if required).

Submitting the completed dissertation

The completed dissertation should be submitted in the form set out by your institution. If there are no formal styles, submit the dissertation in a format that makes it easy for the examiner to handle.

Academic writing

Academic writing requires a certain formality that places the writer in the background and allows the exposition of a carefully worked argument to come to the fore. You may have included statistics, graphs or other representations of data, including multimedia components in your dissertation as well as text. However, in addition to presenting data, your aim is to persuade the reader that you have understood the processes of research and can present that research in a clear and intelligible manner. Acquiring the skills and ability to write academic essays is a developmental process which improves during your studies and should not end with the submission of your dissertation. It is an ongoing process, especially if you want to develop a career in academia. As you develop your academic writing skills, you need to pay attention to the way you write and always present your arguments in a clear, concise and objective formal way

Academic writing is formal. It does not have to be stuffy and complicated, but it does need to be written formally. You will have hopefully learnt the basic skills of academic writing during the production of your undergraduate thesis but just to reinforce the writing style required here are some reminders;

- Avoid using slang, for example: 'the intervention went down a treat', 'the fieldwork was dicey'.
- Don't use contractions. Instead of 'don't', use 'do not'; instead of 'can't' use 'cannot'; instead of 'should've' use 'should have', etc. You'll have noticed that we have used contractions in this book. This is because the norms and conventions are different for study

guides and dissertations. Study guides tend to be less formal than academic essays.

- The same is true for abbreviations. These should also be written out in full:

  - e.g. = for example
  - no. = number
  - i.e. = that is

- You can, however, use recognised acronyms, as long as you define them on their first occurrence:

  - Gross Domestic Product (GDP)
  - Statistics Package for the Social Sciences (SPSS)
  - British National Party (BNP).

- Numbers below 100 should be written in full: eleven participants; forty-nine students. If you use percentages or other units of measurement, however, you can leave them in figures, e.g. 99%.

Always write with clarity, precision and conciseness, avoiding verbosity. In academic discourse avoid the use of words which are subjective and personal. These are statements such as 'very interesting', 'extremely useful', 'excellent'. Such constructions are not used because you cannot be certain whether you and your reader will interpret these words in the same way. Although questions of objectivity or subjectivity are crucial to social science research, the evidence from your research forms the basis of any evaluation rather than through qualifying statements.

Key messages

- Before you start writing your dissertation, draw up a plan of what you need to write and how the chapters or sections will relate to each other. You may wish to add a word count for each chapter.
- Check that the title refers accurately to the finished dissertation. If it does not, change the title.
- Check how your institution wants you to present your work.
- Make sure you explain the significance and relevance of your study in your dissertation.

- Make sure you have enough time to do all the final checking and proofreading of your draft before submitting your dissertation.

Key questions

- Have you structured your dissertation in a logical, coherent and easy to follow way that brings out the points and arguments you are making?
- Does the order of your chapters or sections reflect a good flow of ideas linking all the elements of your study together?
- Have you reviewed relevant academic literature relating to your study and justified your choice of research methodologies you used in your dissertation?
- Have you checked there is a good balance between and within sections or chapters in your dissertation to ensure you have covered the essential areas of your study?
- Have you asked someone to proofread the draft for you to get some feedback before you finally submitted the dissertation?

Further reading

Bell, J. and Waters, S. (2018). *Doing Your Research Project: A Guide for First Time Researchers* (7th Edition). London: Oxford University Press.

Cottrell, S. (2017). *Critical Thinking Skills: Effective Analysis, Argument and Reflection* (3rd Edition). London: Palgrave Macmillan.

Day, T. (2018). *Success in Academic Writing: Palgrave Study Skills*. London: Palgrave Macmillan.

Osmond, A. (2015). *Academic Writing and Grammar for Students* (2nd Edition). London: Sage Publications Ltd.

Chapter 12

Making the most of your dissertation

Introduction

While assessment is the driving reason for doing the dissertation, as a substantive piece of work, the more benefits you can reap from it the better. This chapter explains how a dissertation can be used as a tool to further develop your academic writing skills to enhance your personal development in terms of employment and postgraduate studies. Using your dissertation as a framework to launch a personal development plan, this chapter invites you to reflect on some of the skills you have acquired in the course of your dissertation and how you can use those skills to advance your career in terms of employment.

By the end of this chapter, you will have a better understanding of how to:

- Reflect on and evaluate the essential skills you have acquired through undertaking your dissertation
- Draw on your dissertation success to prepare yourself for the future in relation to job applications and interviews
- Get published and disseminate your dissertation more widely through peer review publications
- Engage in academic research.

What have I got from doing my dissertation?

Your dissertation is probably the longest piece of academic work you have undertaken and are likely to undertake unless you decide to progress to postgraduate study. To successfully complete this work requires a great deal of discipline, self-belief and motivation. It also requires an ability to manage yourself and your time to get the task completed. So, effectively, you have learnt a great deal without even realising it. You have truly developed yourself and learnt about many things that can enhance your career. Not least you have learnt about:

- Time/project management
- Research methods
- Academic writing
- Data collection and analysis techniques
- Formulating and articulating an academic argument.

Your dissertation, therefore, is one piece of work that has enabled you to learn and acquire different skills. You thought about the topic, reviewed existing literature, you formulated your research questions, designed the research, collected the data, analysed the data, tested your hypotheses, evaluated the data, came up with findings and conclusions and wrote the report. All these tasks required a considerable degree of knowledge and understanding of your chosen topic or subject. Through your dissertation you gained a good understanding of how to undertake social research and the challenges of conducting research. Amongst the transferrable skills you have acquired through this process are:

- Project design
- Independent work and initiative
- Time management
- Interpersonal communication
- Data management – collection and analysis
- Critical thinking
- Report writing, etc.

Your dissertation has also given you the skills for dealing with complex social issues that have real life significance or relevance. These transferable skills are what most employers look out for in potential candidates for job interviews. So, based on your dissertation, you need to articulate the skills you have acquired and include these in your CV or any applications for employment or further study.

Graduate attributes and employability

While at university, you will have developed a range of skills and attributes through the learning, teaching and assessment activities that you have experienced, and also through your participation in extra-curricular activities (for example, volunteering, work experience and club memberships). These activities, together with your dissertation, provide an opportunity to reflect on what you have achieved and learned from your degree. Your ability to identify and articulate your strengths and competences will be helpful to you while seeking employment or applying to undertake further studies.

Denholm et al. (2003: 6–7) define four facets to employability that can help you think about what you have learned and how you can make the best use of that learning.

1. Assets (the knowledge, skills and attitudes embodied by the employable graduate).
2. Deployment (the strategies and dispositions of the employable graduate).
3. Presentation (the ability of the graduate to demonstrate their assets and dispositions to employers).
4. Context (the personal and wider social and economic context in which the graduate is seeking work).

Figure 12.1 is a model for an effective self-review approach, showing the interface between personal, career and academic facets to learning.

QAA Scotland (2006) defines eight graduate attributes that may be developed or enhanced through research activities such as your dissertation. These are:

• Critical understanding informed by current developments in the subject;
• An awareness of the provisional nature of knowledge, how knowledge is created, advanced and renewed and the excitement of changing knowledge;
• The ability to identify and analyse problems and issues and to formulate, evaluate and apply evidence-based solutions and arguments;
• An ability to apply a systematic and critical assessment of complex problems and issues;
• An ability to deploy techniques of analysis and enquiry;
• Familiarity with advanced techniques and skills;
• Originality and creativity in formulating, evaluating and applying evidence-based solutions and arguments;
• An understanding of the need for a high level of ethical, social, cultural, environmental and wider professional conduct.

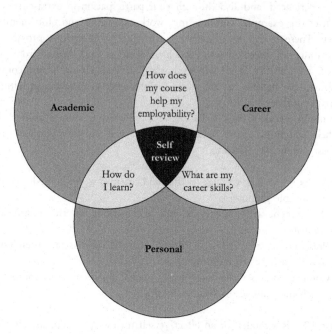

Figure 12.1 Self-review approach (reproduced with permission of QAA)

These attributes may be helpful for you to consider when trying to reflect upon your experience doing your dissertation. Most universities in the UK encourage their undergraduate students to link their dissertation with personal development plans (PDP). 'The process is intended to help individuals understand the value added through learning that is above and beyond attainment in the subjects they have studied' (QAA online).

CV and competence-based interviews

Through an effective CV, you can use the experience of dissertation writing to your advantage when applying for jobs. Competence-based interview techniques are popular, and the type of information requested at the application stage will be competence-based too, so you will want to try to ensure that your application form details and examples you provide are noticed at the interview stage. Your dissertation is about developing skills in research and analysis. When you write your CV, you must show both the evidence of skills you have acquired and demonstrate exactly *how* you have developed these skills and how you will deploy them in the workplace.

In a competence-based interview, you may be asked about *situations* that demonstrate *skills* you have learnt and developed. So, you may wish to use your dissertation to highlight your skills in a range of areas as shown in Figure 12.2.

Dissertation and applications for more advanced levels of study

The research opportunity provided by your dissertation may have led you to consider undertaking further academic study at a higher level. The dissertation might well have sparked a real interest in an area of work that you want to develop further, or you might equally be keen to learn about different approaches to conducting research. You may then be looking for Master's or Doctoral programmes. If this is the case, then, in your application statement, you will need to emphasise your interest and experience of scholarly activity – your dissertation offers a way of evidencing this and supporting a statement. This will be further helped by a reference from your dissertation supervisor.

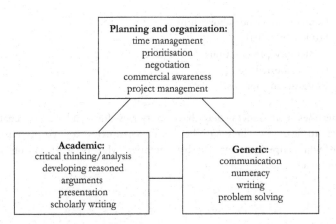

Figure 12.2 Employability skills enhanced through dissertation work

Publishing your dissertation and disseminating your research

Having invested so much time in your dissertation, you may wish to consider disseminating your work more widely than the formal assessment document, particularly if you are interested in a career or further studies in academia. Your research may be relatively modest but have some interest to others beyond those marking it. First you might want to, or have already made a commitment to, sharing your findings with research participants and others who supported your research, for example, if you undertook an organisational case study. You may choose to produce extra copies of the document you submit for assessment. An option that might be more user-friendly and cheaper for you is to produce a short summary report saying what you did, who was involved and what you discovered and/or your key messages. A document of between two and four sides of A4 would be sufficient, in an accessible colour and font type and size. If you want to feed back to younger children or adults with learning disabilities, for example, you might choose to use images to make more impact. There might be occasions when production of a podcast, blog post or short 'talking head' video may be a more appropriate medium through which to share your research findings – a few minutes or less to grip the interest or the audience. Most social media videos are now under two minutes.

Resources and information about publishing dissertations are commonly aimed at doctoral thesis level, but undergraduate dissertations do receive some attention too. Opportunities may include:

- Competitions and scholarships
- Student newsletters
- Conference presentations
- Online journals
- Professional journals.

Sometimes conferences may have bursaries for students to enable them to attend. There might be opportunities for co-presenting with your supervisor or faculty member who is working on the same area.

Case study 12.1 Publishing your dissertation

Case study: *Reinvention: A Journal of Undergraduate Research* published by the Reinvention Centre of Excellence in Teaching and Learning at Warwick University

Dissertations can take months to prepare, but, once marked, even the best are buried away in departmental archives perhaps never to be seen again. To remedy this, a number of journals have arisen which publish exclusively undergraduate research. Foremost among those publishing social science papers is the multidisciplinary *Reinvention: A Journal of Undergraduate Research*. *Reinvention* was launched in 2007 to provide an outlet for undergraduate work and to encourage students to think seriously about conducting original research.

Reinvention considers manuscripts from undergraduates in any intellectual discipline. For many students, a dissertation is their first experience of original research and can be a good opportunity to submit work for publication. However, there are differences between assessed work and an academic paper, and changes are often required to prepare work for publication.

In common with more traditional academic journals, all submissions to *Reinvention* undergo a stringent system of double-blind peer review. Because of this, it can be a useful experience for students to submit their dissertation research for publication. This means that each article is anonymised and sent to two established experts in the field of interest. These reviewers suggest improvements to the article and make recommendations to the editor as to whether it is of a publishable standard. At this point, the editorial team makes a final decision about the article's suitability for publication. If accepted, authors are invited to revise their submission in line with the reviewers' comments. Students whose manuscripts are sent for review may also learn from feedback, which is invariably more detailed than that found on marked coursework. They may also improve their writing style through the process of editing in line with reviewers' comments.

Undergraduate students stand to gain considerably from publishing their work. First, they can learn much about the process of publication; second, publication as a student can greatly boost applications for postgraduate study. It can also suggest to employers that a candidate worked hard and engaged with their

198 Making the most of your dissertation

discipline at university. Furthermore, authors gain recognition for their dissertation efforts and have the opportunity to share their findings with a large audience.

Reinvention is freely accessible by over 1.3 billion internet users via www.go.warwick.ac.uk/reinventionjournal.

Developing your academic writing

If you choose to write for academic publications, you might need to reflect on your own academic writing developed through your dissertation and its further development. However, this may never have been taught to you explicitly. Reading academic textbooks and journal articles, attending lectures and being part of a student community have exposed you to a habit of writing that might be termed 'academic discourse'. Doing your dissertation has equipped you with essential skills to enable you to develop your academic writing. Academic discourse is simply a set of norms and conventions, habits of writing, which make your work intelligible, interesting and engaging to your reader. It assumes that writers and readers form part of a community and can discuss concepts and theories that can be explained, examined and, if necessary, contested, within mutually understood boundaries of communication. As you write more, you will refine your own style, a style which is executed within the boundaries of the social sciences.

Key messages

- Submission is not the end – even if it feels like it on the day you hand your work in.
- Use your dissertation to help you reflect on the wider transferable skills you have acquired through the project.
- Use your dissertation as a springboard for your personal and professional development.
- Make sure you make the most of all the hard work you have put into doing your dissertation by referring to it in your job applications or application for higher studies.

Key questions

- What did you learn from doing your dissertation?
- What aspects of the work did you enjoy the most?

- What are the key skills and knowledge you acquired?
- How might you use these in further study or job applications?
- Would a publication based on your dissertation enhance your job or further study prospects?
- Do you think your dissertation covered a topic or produced some results that would be of interest to others? If yes, why not think about publishing an article based on these?

Further reading

Farenden, J. (2019). Your Dissertation and Employability. CN Career Network. University of Birmingham. [Online] Available at: https://canvas.bham.ac.uk/files/3120670/download?download_frd=1.

Hager, P. and Holland, S. (2006). *Graduate Attributes: Learning and Employability.*. Dordrecht: Springer.

Luey, B. (Ed) (2008). *Revising Your Dissertation: Advice from Leading Editors*. Berkeley: University of California Press..

Reinvention. (2019). Reinvention. An International Journal of Undergraduate Research. Monash-Marwick Alliance, Monash University and Warwick University.. [Online] Available at: www.go.warwick.ac.uk/reinventionjournal.

Appendix I

List of common statistical tests

Statistical tests	Main features
Chi-square	• Applies to data expressed as frequencies. • Measures the discrepancies between the expected and the observed frequencies. • Minimum expected frequencies in any one group must be greater than 5.
Crammer V	• A measure of association for multiple category variables. • Based on Phi coefficient.
Fisher's Exact Probability Test	• A non-parametric test technique. • Used for analysing discrete data (either nominal or ordinal) when the two independent (random) samples are small in size. • Test applies to 2 x 2 tables only.
Goodman-Kruskal	• Measures the proportional reduction in the probability of making an error. • Statistic requires categorical data.
Goodman-Kruskal Tau Tau Tau	• Similar to Goodman-Kruskal Lambda. • Uses a different method for minimising the number of possible errors in predicting from one variable to the other.
Kolmogrov-Smirnov test	• Tests whether two independent samples have been drawn from the same population, or population with the same or similar distributions. • Non-parametric graphical test.
McNemar test and significance	• The McNemar test for the significance of changes. • Applies to 2 x 2 tables only. • Measurement may be nominal or ordinal.

Statistical tests	Main features
Median test and significance	• Tests whether two independent groups differ in central tendencies. • Test evaluates the hypothesis that the groups are drawn from populations having the same median. • Dependent variable must be an ordinal measure.
Pearson C	• Contingency coefficient C – a measure of the extent of association or relation between two sets of attributes.
Pearson r and significance	• Measures the amount of spread about the linear least-squares equation. • Variables must be interval measures. • Coefficient, r ranges from 1.0 to -1.0. • r = 0 indicates no linear association between the variables.
Phi	• A measure of association for 2 x 2 tables.
Sign test and significance	• A non-parametric test used to test the significance of difference between paired variables. • Test is applicable to the case of two related samples when a researcher wishes to establish that two conditions are different. • Variables must be ordinal measure, and the number of categories in variables must be equal.
Spearman's rho and significance	• Measures degree of association. • Requires that both variables be measured in at least an ordinal scale. • Objects may be ranked in two ordered series. • It is applicable to ranked data on the ordinal scale. • Index of correlation (rho) ranges from -1 to +1.
Wilcoxon test and significance	• Test applies to the case of two related samples. • Test differences between two conditions or variables. • Considers the magnitude of differences. • Variables must be measured on interval scale. • Equal number of categories in the variables required.

Appendix 2

Socio-economic deprivation in English towns and cities – 2015

Town/city	Region/country	IMD rank	ID rank	ED rank	HD&D rank	ES&TD rank	Crime rank	BH&S rank	LED rank
Barnsley	Yorkshire and the Humber	30	37	35	26	16	59	95	86
Basildon	East of England	35	21	37	80	1	4	5	99
Basingstoke	South East	106	106	99	103	68	87	59	100
Bath	South West	88	92	87	83	94	98	68	68
Bedford	East of England	66	48	53	74	58	75	12	45
Birkenhead	North West	9	8	2	8	23	29	81	37
Birmingham	West Midlands	5	6	10	34	21	24	1	2
Blackburn	North West	13	16	20	16	10	25	71	21
Blackpool	North West	18	23	25	1	39	9	91	5
Bolton	North West	24	26	23	24	49	26	93	27
Bournemouth	South West	81	87	81	75	86	38	52	35
Bracknell	South East	107	108	106	104	103	107	14	104
Bradford	Yorkshire and the Humber	11	12	22	23	5	2	76	3

Brighton and Hove	South East	69	79	74	63	87	70	17	6
Bristol	South West	62	59	60	62	61	39	40	29
Burnley	North West	19	27	14	5	20	7	96	8
Burton upon Trent	West Midlands	56	71	69	65	34	78	58	13
Bury	North West	55	54	57	52	92	69	97	39
Cambridge	East of England	100	107	105	97	101	97	26	30
Carlisle	North West	64	82	66	27	11	71	74	58
Chatham	South East	47	40	44	86	41	21	21	44
Chelmsford	East of England	95	95	93	96	97	102	28	101
Cheltenham	South West	87	80	85	79	80	51	72	66
Chester	North West	73	66	61	64	74	79	66	74
Chesterfield	East Midlands	68	64	50	29	76	86	67	82
Colchester	East of England	78	75	79	72	71	43	33	78
Coventry	West Midlands	46	46	55	46	62	46	20	22
Crawley	South East	105	103	104	101	67	76	9	105
Darlington	North East	54	42	40	36	65	60	98	96
Derby	East Midlands	43	49	47	54	42	37	78	31
Doncaster	Yorkshire and the Humber	34	31	30	32	28	18	88	53
Dudley	West Midlands	12	3	5	33	4	82	62	32
Eastbourne	South East	82	65	64	78	73	84	49	71
Exeter	South West	84	88	84	88	89	77	64	18

(Continued)

(Cont.)

Town/city	Region/country	IMD rank	ID rank	ED rank	HD&D rank	ES&TD rank	Crime rank	BH&S rank	LED rank
Gateshead	North East	36	29	12	11	37	94	65	87
Gillingham	South East	74	78	76	87	69	47	69	38
Gloucester	South West	67	60	65	61	64	72	29	50
Grimsby	Yorkshire and the Humber	15	14	16	48	6	1	85	23
Guildford	South East	101	98	107	105	98	95	56	81
Halifax	Yorkshire and the Humber	20	22	19	31	35	17	83	4
Harlow	East of England	89	84	89	84	55	31	10	106
Harrogate	Yorkshire and the Humber	102	101	97	94	106	104	77	73
Hartlepool	North East	27	13	7	13	31	52	99	95
Hastings	South East	31	34	34	47	38	32	79	17
Hemel Hempstead	East of England	103	91	102	106	91	92	35	97
High Wycombe	South East	108	105	108	107	95	108	55	88
Huddersfield	Yorkshire and the Humber	51	55	46	66	77	81	70	10
Ipswich	East of England	48	62	63	58	27	62	46	33
Kingston upon Hull	Yorkshire and the Humber	22	24	29	30	13	12	23	19

		23	28	33	21	25	10	36	7
Leeds	Yorkshire and the Humber								
Leicester	East Midlands	39	36	54	53	24	30	61	15
Lincoln	East Midlands	44	44	48	35	66	40	43	36
Liverpool	North West	3	5	6	3	22	27	57	11
London	London	65	56	78	89	104	19	4	16
Luton	East of England	53	51	73	70	82	20	2	55
Maidstone	South East	86	86	86	92	84	74	45	69
Manchester	North West	17	18	31	4	50	5	11	14
Mansfield	East Midlands	32	43	28	38	19	53	47	72
Middlesbrough	North East	7	7	9	14	9	8	94	79
Milton Keynes	South East	77	76	80	85	90	64	8	93
Newcastle upon Tyne	North East	37	35	36	22	36	65	51	89
Newcastle-under-Lyme	West Midlands	80	77	62	56	70	85	100	91
Northampton	East Midlands	57	61	72	60	51	28	7	52
Norwich	East of England	50	50	51	49	52	68	63	48
Nottingham	East Midlands	6	11	21	15	7	11	13	24
Nuneaton	West Midlands	72	70	67	68	59	33	82	56
Oldham	North West	1	2	4	9	3	16	101	65
Oxford	South East	85	85	92	77	85	55	24	46
Peterborough	East of England	29	32	38	43	17	35	25	59

(Continued)

(Cont.)

Town/city	Region/country	IMD rank	ID rank	ED rank	HD&D rank	ES&TD rank	Crime rank	BH&S rank	LED rank
Plymouth	South West	52	57	49	37	57	45	44	26
Poole	South West	94	94	98	93	81	101	39	102
Portsmouth	South East	70	68	82	69	46	44	16	1
Preston	North West	40	52	52	18	54	34	90	20
Reading	South East	90	89	95	99	93	83	32	49
Redditch	West Midlands	58	63	77	67	47	90	3	94
Rochdale	North West	10	9	13	12	14	3	38	76
Rotherham	Yorkshire and the Humber	26	25	18	25	18	14	89	84
Salford	North West	8	20	24	2	12	6	31	25
Scunthorpe	Yorkshire and the Humber	41	38	41	57	26	22	75	64
Sheffield	Yorkshire and the Humber	38	39	42	41	33	48	15	70
Shrewsbury	West Midlands	83	83	83	82	72	103	102	75
Slough	South East	91	93	101	98	100	13	6	62
Solihull	West Midlands	97	99	91	91	108	88	60	90
South Shields	North East	16	10	3	6	48	105	50	107
Southampton	South East	59	67	70	50	53	15	42	12

Southend-on-Sea	East of England	60	58	59	71	63	41	92	43
Southport	North West	79	81	58	55	102	99	103	51
St Albans	East of England	109	109	109	108	109	109	48	83
St Helens	North West	14	19	11	7	45	54	104	47
Stevenage	East of England	96	96	94	100	60	80	41	108
Stockport	North West	75	74	71	42	83	49	105	54
Stockton-on-Tees	North East	33	30	26	20	30	42	106	92
Stoke-on-Trent	West Midlands	21	33	27	19	15	23	84	40
Sunderland	North East	28	15	15	10	32	89	107	103
Sutton Coldfield	West Midlands	98	100	96	102	107	106	30	77
Swindon	South West	76	72	68	76	56	56	86	80
Telford	West Midlands	42	41	39	40	44	57	27	109
Wakefield	Yorkshire and the Humber	49	45	43	39	40	63	87	63
Walsall	West Midlands	4	4	8	45	8	36	34	9
Warrington	North West	63	69	56	44	75	66	80	60
Watford	East of England	99	97	100	95	96	96	19	67
West Bromwich	West Midlands	2	1	1	17	2	50	22	28
Weston-Super-Mare	South West	61	53	45	59	78	73	53	61
Wigan	North West	45	47	32	28	43	58	108	85
Woking	South East	104	102	103	109	105	100	54	98
Wolverhampton	West Midlands	25	17	17	51	29	61	37	57

(Continued)

(Cont.)

Town/city	Region/country	IMD rank	ID rank	ED rank	HD&D rank	ES&TD rank	Crime rank	BH&S rank	LED rank
Worcester	West Midlands	71	73	75	73	79	67	18	34
Worthing	South East	92	104	90	81	99	91	109	42
York	Yorkshire and the Humber	93	90	88	90	88	93	73	41

N.B.

IMD – Index of Multiple Deprivation
This is an overall measure of multiple deprivation experienced by people living in an area as calculated for every Lower-layer Super Output Area (LSOA) in England. LSOAs are areas averaging a population of around 1,500 or 650 households. Every LSOA in England was ranked according to its level of deprivation relative to that of other areas.
ID – Income Deprivation
ED – Employment Deprivation
HD&D – Health Deprivation and Disability
ES&TD - Education, Skills and Training Deprivation
BH&S - Barriers to Housing and Services
LED - Living Environment Deprivation

Source: Office for National Statistics licensed under the Open Government Licence.

References

Allen, D. (2015). *Getting Things Done: The Art of Stress-free Productivity*. Little, Brown, London.

Antonio, A. and Tuffley, D. (2014). The Gender Digital Divide in Developing Countries. *Future Internet*, 6, 673–687.

Banks, M. (2007) *Using Visual Data in Qualitative Research*. Sage, London.

Baptiste, I. (2001). Qualitative data analysis: Common phases, strategic differences [Electronic Version]. *Forum: Qualitative Social Research*, 2(3). www.qualitative-research.net/fqs-texte/3-01/3-01baptiste-e.htm. Retrieved 10 October 2007.

Beissel-Durrant, G. (2004) *A Typology of Research Methods within the Social Sciences*. National Centre for Research Methods, Southampton.

Bhattacherjee, A. (2012). *Social Science Research: Principles, Methods, and Practices* (2nd Edition). University of South Florida, Tampa, FL.

Bhattacherjee, A., and Premkumar, G. (2004). Understanding changes in belief andattitude toward information technology usage: A theoretical model and longitudinal test. *MIS Quarterly*, 28, 229–254.

Bolderston, A. (2008). Writing an Effective Literature Review. *Journal of Medical Imaging an Radiation Sciences*. [Online]. Available at: https://scs.msu.edu/sa/wfp/files-addtl/Writing%20an%20Effective%20Literature%20Review%20(Amanda%20Bolderston).pdf. Accessed 12 May 2019.

Brannen, J. (2005) *Mixed Methods Research: A Discussion Paper*. National Centre for Research Methods, Southampton.

Bryman, A. (2004). *Social Research Methods* (2nd Edition). Oxford University Press, Oxford.

Cayli, B., Hargreaves, C. and Hodgson, P. (2018) "Body-worn cameras: determining the democratic habitus of policing", *Safer Communities*, 17 (4), 213–223.

Chandler, D. (1994) 'Semiotics for Beginners', available online at www.aber.ac.uk/media/Documents/S4B (accessed 29 April 2008).

Churches, R. and Dommett, E. (2016) *Teacher-Led Research*. Crown House, Wales, Camarthen.

Copus, J. (2010). *Brilliant Writing Tips for Students*. Basingstoke: Palgrave Macmillan.

Cottrell, S. (2014). *Dissertations and Project Reports A Step by Step Guide*. Basingstoke: Palgrave Macmillan.

Cottrell, S. (2017). *Critical Thinking Skills: Effective Analysis, Argument and Reflection* (3rd Edition). Palgrave Macmillan, Basingstoke.

Critical Appraisal Skills Programme (CASP). Qualitative Research Checklist. [Online] Available at: http://media.wix.com/ugd/dded87_29c5b002d99342f788c6ac670e49f274.pdf. Accessed 16 June 2019.

Dawson, C. (2019). *Introduction to Research Methods*. A Practical Guide for Anyone Undertakling a Research Project (5th Edition). Little, Brown Book Group, London.

Day, T. (2018). *Success in Academic Writing. Palgrave Study Skills*. Palgrave Macmillan, London.

Denholm, J., Mcleod, D., Boyes, L. and McCormick, J. (2003) *Higher Education: Higher Ambitions? Graduate Employability in Scotland*. Critical Thinking, Policy Works, Scottish Council, Edinburgh.

Denney, A. S., and Tewksbury, R. (2013). How to write a literature review. *Journal of Criminal Justice Education*, 24, 218–234.

Denzin, N. K. and Lincoln, Y. S. (2011). *The Sage Handbook of Qualitative Research* (4th Edition). Sage, London.

Elsbach, K. and Stigliani, I. (2018). New Information Technologies and Implicit Bias. *Journal of Academy of Management Perspectives*, 33 (2), 185–206. Published Online: https://doi.org/10.5465/amp.2017.0079; Accessed 9th December 2019.

Embree, L. (1997) *Encyclopedia of Phenomenology*. Kluwer Academic Publishers, Boston, MA.

Ezzy, D. (2002) *Qualitative Research: Practice and Innovation*. Routledge, London.

Fairclough, N. (2003) *Analysing Discourse: Textual Analysis for Social Research*. Routledge, London.

Forsyth, P. (2016). *How to Write Reports and Proposals* (4th Edition). Kogan Page, London.

Gee, J.P. (2005) *An Introduction to Discourse Analysis: Theory and Method*. Routledge, London.

Gibbs, G. (2007) *Analysing Qualitative Data*. Sage, London.

Glaser, B. and Strauss, A. (1967) *The Discovery of Grounded Theory: Strategies for Qualitative Research*. Weidenfeld & Nicolson, London.

Gobo, G. and Marciniak, L. (2016). What Is Ethnography? In D. Silverman (Ed). *Qualitative Research*. Sage, London, pp. 103–120.

Godfrey, J. (2010). *Reading and Making Notes* (2nd Edition). Pocket Study Skills. Palgrave Macmillan, London.

Godfrey, J. (2011). *Writing for University*. Pocket Study Skills. Palgrave Macmillan, London.

Hargreaves, C, Hodgson, P, Noor Mohamed, J and Nunn, A. (2018) Contingent coping? Re-negotiating 'fast' disciplinary social policy at street level: implementing the UK troubled families programme. *Critical Social Policy*, 39 (2), 289–308.

Harrington, K., O'Neill, P., and Bakhshi, S. (2007) Writing Mentors and the Writing Centre: producing integrated disciplinary writers. Investigations in University Teaching and Learning, 4, 26–32.

Harzing, A-W. (2018) How to keep up to date with the literature but avoid information overload, [Online] Available at: http://blogs.lse.ac.uk/impactofsocials ciences/2018/05/18/how-to-keep-up-to-date-with-the-literature-but-avoid-infor mation-overload/

Hutchinson, D. (2014) WMA Declaration of Helsinki 2013: Ethical Principles for Medical Research Involving Human Subjects. Canary Publications. 1st edition (1 Feb. 2014).

Huot, S. (2014). Ethnography – Understanding Occupation through an Examination of Culture. In S. Naylor and M. Stanley (Eds). *Qualitative Research Methodologies for Occupational Science and Therapy.* Taylor & Francis, Hoboken, NJ, pp. 84–100.

Jones, J. and Smith, J. (2017). Ethnography: Challenges and Opportunities. *Evidence-Based Nursing*, 20 (4), 98–100.

Kandlbinder, P. and Peseta, T. (2006) *In Supervisors' Words: An Insider's View of Postgraduate Supervision.* Institute for Teaching and Learning, University of Sydney, Sydney.

Kuhn, T. (1970) *The Structure of Scientific Revolutions* (2nd Edition). University of Chicago Press, Chicago.

Kumar, R. (2014). *Research Methodology: A Step-b-step Guide for Beginners.* Sage, London.

Lawler, S. (2002) 'Narrative in Social Research', in T. May (ed.) *Qualitative Research in Action.* Sage, London.

Lawrence, C. (2011). Writing a Literature Review in the Social Sciences. [Online] Available at www.academia.edu/2911352/Writing_a_Literature_Review_in_the_ Social_Sciences. Accessed on 11th May 2019.

Luey, B. (Ed) (2004).*Revising Your Dissertation: Advice from Leading Editors.* University of California Press, Berkeley, CA.

Marchant-Shapiro, T. (2015). *Statistics for Political Analysis.* Sage, London.

Markham, A. and Buchanan, E. (2012): Ethical Decision-Making and Internet Research. Association of Internet Researchers, Ethics Working Committee, (AoIR 2012).

Marsen, S. (2013). *Professional Writing* (3rd Edition). *Palgrave Study Skills.* Palgrave McMillan, London.

McMillan, K. and Weyers, J. (2011): *How to Write Dissertations & Project Reports* (2nd Edition). Pearson Education Limited, Edinburgh Gate, Harlow, England.

McMillan, K. and Weyers, J. (2012). *How to Cite Reference & Avoid Plagiarism at University.* Pearson, Harlow, England.

Miles, M. B. and Huberman, A. M. (1994) *Qualitative Data Analysis* (2nd Edition). Sage, London.

Miller, R. L. and Brewer, J. D. (2003) *The A—Z of Social Research.* Sage, London.

Neale, J. (2016). Iterative Categorization (IC): A Systematic Technique for Analysing Qualitative Data. *Adiction*, 111 (6), 1096–1106. Published by John Wiley & Sons on behalf of the Society for the Study of Addiction, 9th May 2016.

Neuman, W. L. (2006). *Social research methods: Qualitative and quantitative approaches*. Pearson Education Inc, New York.

O'Leary, Z. (2018). *Research Proposal*. Sage, London.

Panda, J. and Alekya, P. (2018). How to Conduct an Effective Literature Review and Its Management. *International Journal of Education and Psychological Research (IJEPR)*, 7 (3), 3–41. September 2018.

Patel, S. (2015). The Research Paradigm – Methodology, Epistemology and Ontology – Explained in Simplelanguage. [Online] Available at: http://salmapa tel.co.uk/academia/the-research-paradigm-methodology-epistemology-and-ontol ogy-explained-in-simple-language/. Accessed 5th May 2019.

Pauwel, L. (2011). An Integrated Conceptual Framework for Visual Social Research. In E. Margolis and L. Pauwels (Eds). *The Sage Handbook of Visual Research Methods*. Sage, London.

Potter, J. (2004) 'Discourse Analysis as a Way of Analysing Naturally Occurring Talk', in D. Silverman (ed.) *Qualitative Research: Theory, Method and Practice*. Sage, London, pp. 200–221.

Prosser, J. (2006) 'Working Paper: Researching with Visual Images: Some Guidance Notes and a Glossary for Beginners', *Real Life Methods*, ESRC National Centre for Research Methods Working Paper series 6/06. Available online at www.ncrm.ac.uk/research/outputs/publications/WorkingPapers/2006/ 0606_researching_visual_images.pdf (accessed 24 April 2008).

QAA (2006) 'Enhancement Themes', available online at www.enhancement-themes.ac.uk/themes/employability (accessed 20 July 2008).

Ritchie, J., Lewis, J. and McNaughton-Nichols, C., (2013). *Qualitative Research Practice: A Guide for Social Science Students and Researchers* (2nd Edition). Sage, London.

Robson, C. (2014). *How to Do a Research Project: A Guide for Undergraduate Students* (2nd Edition). Chichester: Wiley.

Rowena, M. (2017). *How to Write a Thesis* (4th Edition). Open University Press, Maidenhead, Berkshire, UK.

Swales, J. M. and Feak, C. B. (2004) *Academic Writing for Graduate Students: Essential Tasks and Skills*. University of Michigan Press, Ann Arbor, MI.

Thomas, G. (2017). *Doing Research* (2nd Edition). Red Globe Press, Macmillan International.

Todd, M. J., Smith, K. and Bannister, P. (2006) 'Staff Experiences and Perceptions of Supervising a Social Science Undergraduate Dissertation', *Teaching in Higher Education*, 11 (2), 161–173.

Todd, M., Bannister, P. and Clegg, S. (2004) 'Independent Inquiry and the Undergraduate Dissertation: Perceptions and Experiences of Final Year Social Science Students', *Assessment and Evaluation in Higher Education*, 29, 335–355.

Tong, A., Sainsbury, P. and Craig, J. (2007). Consolidated Criteria for Reporting Qualitative Research (COREQ): A 32-item Checklist for Interviews and Focus Groups. *International Journal for Quality in Health Care*, 19 (6), 349–357.

Van der Velde, N., Jansen, P. and Anderson, N. (2004) *Guide to Management Research Methods*. Blackwell, Oxford.

Walliman, N. (2013) *Your Undergraduate Dissertation: The Essential Guide for Success*. London: Sage.

Weber, S. (2008) 'Visual Images in Research', in J.G. Knowles and A.L. Cole (eds), *Handbook of the Arts in Qualitative Research: Perspectives, Methodologies, Examples, and Issues*. Sage, London, pp. 41–53.

WhatIs.com. EA in Transition: Guide to Keeping up with Disruptive Technologies. [Online] Available at: http://whatis.techtarget.com/definition/social-media. Accessed 2 May 2019.

Williams, K. (2017). *Referencing and Understanding Plagiarism*. Palgrave Macmillan, Basingstoke.

Winstanley, C. (2010). *Writing a Dissertation for Dummies*. John Wiley & Sons., Chichester.

Wright, C. (2016). *Social Media for Researchers*. National Co-ordinating Centre for Public Engagement. Sage Publishing, April 2016.

Index

Locators in **bold** refer to tables and those in *italics* to figures.